ISBN 978-1-331-18231-3
PIBN 10155132

1 MONTH OF
FREE
READING

at

www.ForgottenBooks.com

By purchasing this book you are eligible for one month membership to ForgottenBooks.com, giving you unlimited access to our entire collection of over 1,000,000 titles via our web site and mobile apps.

To claim your free month visit:

www.forgottenbooks.com/free155132

English
Français
Deutsche
Italiano
Español
Português

www.forgottenbooks.com

Mythology Photography **Fiction**
Fishing Christianity **Art** Cooking
Essays Buddhism Freemasonry
Medicine **Biology** Music **Ancient
Egypt** Evolution Carpentry Physics
Dance Geology **Mathematics** Fitness
Shakespeare **Folklore** Yoga Marketing
Confidence Immortality Biographies
Poetry **Psychology** Witchcraft
Electronics Chemistry History **Law**
Accounting **Philosophy** Anthropology
Alchemy Drama Quantum Mechanics
Atheism Sexual Health **Ancient History**
Entrepreneurship Languages Sport
Paleontology Needlework Islam
Metaphysics Investment Archaeology
Parenting Statistics Criminology
Motivational

JOHN SOBIESKI OR JOHN III
KING OF POLAND

THE LIFE OF KING JOHN SOBIESKI

John the Third of Poland

A CHRISTIAN KNIGHT
THE SAVIOR OF CHRISTENDOM

BY

COUNT JOHN SOBIESKI

*Author of A Soldier of Freedom, The Adventures of a
Polish Nobleman While Fighting Under the
Flag of Two Republics, and The
Life of President Juarez.*

ARTI et VERITATI

BOSTON: RICHARD G. BADGER
TORONTO: THE COPP CLARK CO., LIMITED

1915

The Gorham Press, Boston, U. S. A.

and crushing and the Turks were compelled to return to their own homes. The Grand Marshal (John Sobieski) then ascended the throne of Poland as John the Third.

In the spring of 1683 the King of Poland was reported to be suffering from an incurable disease which would prevent him ever taking to the field of battle again at the head of his troops, and, as cited above, the Christian nations were at swords points. To make matters still more serious, Hungaria, suffering from the oppression of Austria, stood ready to furnish fifty thousand of its best troops (in order to avenge herself) to assist the Porte in his operations against Austria, so that a very great army was assembled, and marched triumphantly to the very gates of Vienna and the Porte laid siege to that city, and in the very hour when victory seemed sure, Sobieski suddenly appeared with an army of only seventy thousand men and struck the Turks like a whirlwind. The Turks were so dumbfounded and bewildered by his sudden movement that they fled, panic-stricken, so that the proud, exultant foe was scattered to the winds, leaving behind them all of their war materials, and never stopping until they had reached the borders of Hungaria. Thus ended forever the Mohammedan Power as a military force.

This defeat was so final that it was the very end of the Oriental dream of supremacy in Europe, and by this victory Sobieski's name stands with the highest in military annals. His ability certainly exceeded Marlborough of England, Frederick of Prussia, and was only equaled by Napoleon, never excelled, for he never was defeated in any great battle.

The purpose of this volume is to introduce this great Christian warrior and king more thoroughly to the English-speaking world, that he may be known and appreciated as the great ruler who, more than any other, saved Europe to Christian civilization.

JOHN SOBIESKI.

Los Angeles, Calif.
February, 1915.

THE LIFE OF KING JOHN SOBIESKI

THE LIFE OF KING
JOHN SOBIESKI

CHAPTER I

IN the year sixteen twenty-nine (1629), when Sigismund the Third reigned in Poland, Louis the Thirteenth in France, Charles the First in England, and the Snow King, so called in history, the celebrated Gustavus Adolphus in Sweden, was born John Sobieski in the castle of Olensko, a town in the palatinate of Russia. Sobieski was descended from two of the greatest families of Poland whose origin the Polish genealogists have placed far back in the obscure ages of antiquity. It is a truth of greater, or much easier proved, certainty that these families were renowned for their virtue and patriotism.

The renowned Zolkiewski, grandfather of Sobieski on the mother's side, defeated the Muscovites in 1610, and the Czar was made a prisoner and was brought to the capital of Cracow. Monuments of this victory are still seen upon the ceilings of the castle at Warsaw. When Czar Peter was called into Poland to defend King Augustus against Charles the Twelfth, the Czar thought proper to destroy them, but the testimony of time cannot be suppressed. In the year 1620 Zolkiewski forced his way through a hundred thousand Turks and Tartars, who surrounded him in Moldavia, and was retreating before this great host which pursued and harassed him during a march of almost a hundred leagues. Having reached the frontiers of Poland upon the banks of the Niester, his cavalry, now completely exhausted, was apparently looking into the face of certain destruction, so they took the first opportunity of escape, which was to swim across the river, thus deserting their general and his infantry. Zolkiewski's son, who was with him in the army, begged him to consider his own safety, but he replied that the Republic had entrusted its entire army to him and he could not desert it. The infantry that remained was utterly annihilated before his eyes; his brave son expired in his sight. He himself was covered with wounds and lived but a short time. His head was severed by the Turkish general and sent to the Sultan to revive the spirits of the Ottoman Empire, but was afterwards redeemed and the renowned father and son buried in the same grave. Upon their tomb was this inscription: "May our avenger rise out of our ashes."

The work of avenging these two noble souls was

reserved for one Sobieski, their descendant from the female line, who never read without emotion that inscription which exhorted to vengeance.

John Sobieski's father's father, Mark Sobieski, palatine of Lublin, left his grandson many great exploits to copy. Came to him the happy event of the battle in which Michael, hospodar of Moldavia, was defeated. Also he had his grandfather's example in the part he took in the defeat of the rebellious Dantzickers in 1577, when he threw himself into the waters of the Vistula in pursuit of their leader, and when he came upon him slew him with his own hands in the midst of the river; which action was performed in the presence of the King, who declared that if it should ever be necessary to risk the fate of Poland in a single combat, as the fortunes of Rome were once entrusted to Horatius, he should not for a single moment hesitate to choose the palatine of Lublin as her defender. The brave palatine was killed at the attack of Sokol, a Russian fortress, which the Poles took by storm, and such was the grandfather of John Sobieski and the military heritage he was enriched with.

His father, James Sobieski, was not unworthy of such a noble sire, as subsequent history of valorous deeds tells us. One of the most glorious victories in all the annals of Poland was the famous battle of Choczin, in 1622, in which the young Prince Uladislas, son of King Sigismund III, had the title of commander-in-chief, but the one who was entitled to the glory of the victory was James Sobieski, who had taken command in the absence of the Grand-General. Two hundred thousand Turks and Tartars were defeated in that battle by sixty-five thousand Poles, and the hero of the day, being as able a negotiator or diplomat as he was a general on the field, was sent by the King as his ambassador to sign the treaty which the Porte was compelled to accept. By his (James Sobieski's) marriage with the daughter of the great Zolkiewski, and heiress of the vast estates in the possession of that powerful family, palatinate of Russia, he had two sons, Mark and John, whose education he considered encumbered upon himself, and held definite ideas regarding the education of young people which were not shared by all his contemporaries. He instructed them in the principles of justice, beneficence and respect for the established laws of the land, holding that a knowledge of these things was as important as a knowledge of military tactics, and as unsurpassed, even, by military glory in which each and every one hoped to shine. He gradually led them up to the vital interests of their native land, their beloved Poland, and instructed them to defend these interests by written as well as spoken words, all of which would be useless under an absolute form of government but necessary in a republic. James Sobieski labored to instill in his sons that habit of application which he, himself, possessed and without which there can never be great men.

The eldest son, Mark, was of mild temper and docile disposition, his mother's favorite, and, had he lived, would have been compelled to occupy a subordinate place to his younger brother, John Sobieski.

John Sobieski was of a lively, ardent and impetuous temper, with great executive ability and will power, determined to accomplish that which he undertook to do. If there were in existence any adequate history of his childhood, we should, undoubtedly, be able to discover the characteristics which afterwards made him the greatest king and soldier of his day.

There is one characteristic of the Polish people which has existed from the dawn of their history and that is that a Pole does not believe that he possesses, exclusively, everything of value or that he can learn nothing outside his own country, so that the Poles stand out in strong contrast to other nationalities of that day; consequently, to receive an education that should be complete in every detail, the two sons, Mark and John, started out upon extensive travels which took them first to France, for even at that early day France, in matters of culture and refinement, stood at the head of the world. The boys, almost young men now, remained in France long enough to become thoroughly versed in the language of that country. The younger brother became such a master of languages, eventually, that he spoke six, each of which might have been taken for his mother tongue. After visiting the great capitals of Europe, the last place they visited was Constantinople, that they might become better acquainted with that power. Little did the Porte imagine that a day would come when his army was to flee before the younger of these brothers.

Being now conversant with what knowledge they could collect in Europe and in Constantinople, the gateway to Europe, they determined to penetrate into Asia, but just as they were setting forth upon this journey they learned that a war had broken out on the frontier of Poland. They returned at once to tender their services in behalf of their country but, alas, they had not the satisfaction of being received in the embrace of a father who had cared for them and educated them, for he had passed away, leaving his sons, however, the memory of a noble father as a splendid inheritance.

The throne of Poland was, at that time, 1648, filled by Casimir V, who had risen from a cardinal to a king. He was now upon the point of seeing the scepter wrested from his hands. Gloomy indeed was that age for the crowned heads of Europe. The

Thirty Years' War, the greatest strife in which Europe had been embroiled since the days of the Roman invasions, had just ended and the fact that the Thirty Years' War was not only a religious war which had grown out of the foment which Martin Luther had caused to start, but that it was a war to preserve a certain balance of power with the great principalities eying, enviously and greedily, no doubt, the very evident plan of Austria to make of Vienna a religious power which had known no equal save that of Rome, is a truth which must be remembered, for upon that, beyond the question of a doubt, was one of the gravest reasons for continuing the power of the Catholic faith as against the Protestant and of adding to that faith against the invasions of the Turks who were, at that time, a very powerful foe. So we repeat, that the age was indeed a gloomy one for the rulers of Europe. Philip the Fourth had lost Portugal and the most of his possessions in Asia. In France the mother of Louis the Fourteenth had been forced out of Paris with her children. In England, after a long struggle with his parliament, Charles the First had died upon the scaffold. The inglorious flight of the Polish army at Pilawiecz was but recent, when the two Sobieskis arrived in Poland. Their mother, a woman of noble spirit, exclaimed as soon as she saw them —" Are you come to avenge your country? I renounce you forever as

my sons if you behave like the combatants at Pilawiecz!" How well they fought the records attest.
The Poles were defeated in two pitched battles, and
in the last of these Mark, the younger Sobieski, was
slain in the very flower of his age.

CHAPTER II

WHAT had been done by John Sobieski, now at the head of his family (1649), was but a prelude to his future exploits in war. All that had been observed in him, up to this time, was an impetuous ardor which made him reckless of danger and which carried him where the mere sense of duty would not require his presence. A single event displays the credit which he had acquired in so short a time. When the Polish army mutinied in the camp at Sborow, a city of Little Poland up on the borders of Podolia, and every method, such as persuasion to which was added menace and even cannon of the Lithuanian troops, had been tried in vain by the commanding general, and the attempt given up as hopeless, John Sobieski asked that he might try what he could do in inducing the men to return to their duties. The temerity of extraordinary men is never justified but by the success that attends it. It is easy to understand what address and eloquence are needed to pursuade men who had arms in their hands. It is not only a matter of personal pride, but it is a racial pride which every true Pole feels when we find that Sobieski, a very

young man as we look upon men today, with his
grace of eloquence carried his point and thus early
showed that empire over the minds of men which
would have done credit to a consummate general and
this feat advanced to the height of glory a youth who
had, as yet, held no public office. He not only, by
his wondrous eloquence, persuaded those mutineers
to return to their duty, but he filled them with a new
spirit of loyalty and enthusiasm for their country
and its cause.

The army advanced now upon the foe in a spirit
that can never fail of victory. The battle lasted
seven days and the loss of the enemy was twenty
thousand men. A peace was obtained that was in
every way satisfactory to the Republic, which had
become embroiled, through her weak and vacillating
king, in so much useless slaughter. The immediate
result to Sobieski was that he was rewarded by being
made the great Standard-bearer of the Crown, an
officer of the Court and of the army, who carries the
banner of the Republic at the coronations and at the
funerals of the Kings of Poland. This was a remarkable rise in a republic which, at this critical
time in its national history, must be, or should have
been, careful how it proceeds and should confer re-
wards rather than favors. However, the promotion
of Sobieski was both in the nature of a reward and
was also one of those marks of favor which fate had

reserved for him.

Poland now saw, as she had not seen for a long time, a great number of enemies united (1655) to conspire her ruin. Christiana of Sweden had resigned her crown and had gone to Rome to spend the rest of her days in arts and letters in preference to remaining with her own people and endeavoring to further the happiness of her kingdom. She was succeeded by her cousin, Charles Gustavus, who made the same mistake that so many others have made, and that was in thinking that the most effective way of showing his ability to reign was to enter upon a war of conquest, a part of which is due to the period in which he lived when the conscience that Europe found living within itself and her growing pains of reformation, were, after all, secondary to the old race idea that might makes right. In a brief time, with the aid of allies, Charles Gustavus, had made himself master of a great part of Poland and proceeded to make war upon Prussia.

Any other than the weak king who ruled Poland would have seen his mistake in antagonizing some who should have been his friends rather than enemies.

Sobieski, although he served in an army that was everywhere defeated, was yet learning to conquer. If Casimir had had many Sobieskis he might have escaped the sad extremity to which he was reduced.

Gustavus was already advancing upon him from Prussia. Sobieski blocked him up between the Vistula and the Sanus, hindered him being supplied with provisions and harassed him with continual skirmishes. Receiving information that one Swedish general was approaching with six thousand men to relieve the King, Sobieski left his little army to continue the blockade while he marched with his cavalry to meet Douglas, the Swedish general. He forded the Pilcza, a river much swollen by the melting snows, and with that alacrity which characterized all of his movements and was, in reality, the secret of his success, he surprised Douglas, delivered a crushing defeat to that general, and followed his fleeting army to the very suburbs of Warsaw.

Some parts of the Polish army which had been depended upon to do their duty in this emergency failed entirely, so that it was necessary to make another division to meet and oppose Ragotski, the Prince of Transylvania, who advanced in concert with the Swedish forces with the intention of depriving Casimir of the throne. Surrounded by so many enemies, it is not surprising that some blunders were made and less surprising that the King of Sweden should take advantage of them, which he did and succeeded in extricating himself from the position where Sobieski had placed him. He now advanced toward Warsaw where a general engagement took place. The battle lasted three days and it was a battle well fought, with tremendous energy on both sides, so that the field was red with blood and covered with the mangled bodies of the slain, but still again the arms of the King of Sweden were victorious. The Republic of Poland would have been utterly ruined by these stunning defeats but that, at this juncture, the allied forces, led by the King of Sweden, were deprived of that great leader by death. Thus ended the career of Charles Gustavus, one of the most brilliant men of his time. He was but little, if any, inferior to the great Gustavus Adolphus, his uncle, and doubtless, had he been spared, he would have been recorded as one of the world's greatest generals, for a longer life might, and no doubt would, have given him the opportunity to restore the exchequer of his country to an adequacy of demands.

Ragotski, who succeeded Charles Gustavus, was a man of great ambition, but an ambition that was not equaled in talents. He disregarded the advice of Charles Gustavus to follow and annihilate Lubomirski, one of the generals of the Polish army, and Sobieski made an incursion into his territory where he committed the same hostilities that had afflicted Poland. Ragotski succeeded in defending himself no better than he had done in attacking others, and was glad to accept of a humiliating peace after which he never disturbed his neighbors. Sweden, herself, no longer financially able to carry on an exhausting war, was glad to make the peace for which her late King was also more than willing, as there had been no perceptible gain for all the terrible cost and the awful sacrifice of men.

Poland still had two near enemies with whom to deal: the Muscovites and Cossacks, the latter of whom she had needlessly animated to a degree of animosity by cruel oppression. It was of the utmost importance to prevent the Muscovites and the Cossacks joining forces, but to prevent this there was needed a man of great ability. Sobieski was selected, and, with the celerity of lightning, he moved upon them and attacked them upon their arrival at the Ukraine, where he delivered them a stunning blow and a terrible defeat. His victory was complete in every detail. The Cossack general was taken prisoner, put in chains and sent to the Polish King. This brilliant victory over the Cossacks very naturally filled the Muscovites with fear and trembling, and they surrendered their army without fighting.

Nothing now remained but to recapture a few places in Lithuania, one of which was Wilna, one of Poland's most important cities, built entirely of wood for the want of stone. The Muscovite general who commanded the citadel would have put any man to death who would even have talked of surrendering. He had suspicions of a Polish priest and put him into a mortar and discharged this frightful and gruesome bomb upon the besiegers. His ' brutality, cruelty, and obstinacy, joined to the impossibility of making a long defense, caused the foreign officers in the garrison to rise in mutiny against the Muscovite commander. They surrendered, thus, both the city and the citadel into the hands of the besiegers. The Poles, having gotten the Muscovite barbarian general into their hands and power, condemned him to die at the hands of a common executioner, but none being found the general's own cook offered, no doubt to repay some old grudge, to do the deed and was permitted to cut the head off his master. It is not difficult to realize what manner of man the master was who had in his employ such a servant.

Lubomirski, being in disgrace, was deposed from royal favor. Czarneski, Palatine of Kiovia, was made petty general and Sobieski, for his brilliant victories, was promoted to the dignity of Grand Marshal, a post of high distinction, but a civil position having no military authority or jurisdiction.

In order to clearly understand the form of government it may not be unwise to pause for a brief survey. The Republic had four great officers who were entrusted with the four principal, or primary, branches of the administration. The Grand General directed the affairs of the army; this is similar to the Secretary of War in modern Republics. The Grand

Chancellor presided over the administration of justice and was similar to the Chief Justice of the United States or the Lord Chief Justice of England. The next was the Grand Treasurer, whose position was not synonomous with the Secretary of the Treasury in the United States, but quite similar. It fell to his lot to devise means of raising revenues for the support of the government both in time of peace and for purposes of warfare. Next was the Grand Marshal who was, in fact, a national chief of police. These four personages were called Brachia Regalia, that is, Arms of the King.

Lubomirski rebelled at what he considered the injustice which had been done him, and resolved to obtain justice by dint of arms. He, therefore, entered Poland at the head of an army of less than a thousand men, but soon found himself at the head of an army of five thousand strong. The King assembled a superior force and detached the Lithuanian contingency, commanded by Polubinski, to attack the rebel army, but the rebels defeated the royalists and took a great number of prisoners, Polubinski being among them. The conqueror treated them with all the humanity that could have been expected of a friend and dismissed them without a ransom. But his treatment of Sobieski was not so generous, for he ravished his estates, and carried off his cattle. However, the temptation to crush the rival who has been raised up upon one's own ruin is a temptation that few can resist.

The success of the rebel leader opened up before him Great Poland and while the royal army was exerting every effort to stop his passage, the nobility, which had at first either openly opposed him or had simply refused to take sides, now found it convenient to espouse the cause of Lubomirski, and for a while the skies looked dark for the Republic.

Two Senators, who were bishops, induced the two armies to continue in sight of each other without coming to an engagement until the holding of a special session of the diet which the King had called to meet in Warsaw on the seventeenth of March. This action gave hopes to Lubomirski of his restoration and to his army of the pay it required.

Lubomirski, being of a warm, generous nature, was ready to forgive an injury as soon as satisfaction was made and did not disdain, though victorious, to appear in the form of suppliant. At last the great day which kept both armies in suspense arrived. The Marshal of the Deputies, who acted as speaker, enlarged in vague terms upon the advantages of peace; the moment was supposed to be come which would produce Lubormirski and his interests upon the stage, but the orator who kept his eye fixed upon the King had not the courage to enter the subject and a vote, which issued from the midst of the assemblage, put an end to the address and the diet together.

The King's anger, which grew more and more inflamed, encountered a new obstacle in the way of Lubomirski's restoration. Czarneski, who had succeeded him as general, was dead and the King had appointed Sobieski to the post. The King, by this step, had put himself in an embarrassing situation and the consequence of it was that the war recommenced with greater fury than before.

The King, heading an army of twenty-six thousand men, marched in search of the enemy of eighteen thousand. The two factions approached near each other on the thirteenth day of July in the palatinate of Cijavia. This was the first occasion that Sobieski acted as general. There was a morass intervening between the two armies which the King ordered him to pass. Sobieski explained to the King the danger of such a project, it being easy to see that the enemy would suffer only such a number to pass as they could conquer, but the King refused to regard the remonstrance, and ordered Sobieski to assume his command. The King's troops entered the morass, were soon embedded in the mud and only succeeded in crossing with the greatest difficulty.

Besides being animated by their countries' interests, which both sides claimed, at the same time evincing a willingness to tear one another to pieces, there was perpetual hatred between the two opposing generals, both of whom were not only brave in action, but gifted in the arts and learned in the skill of warfare. One general, newly appointed to office, attacked another who had been degraded and dishonored to make room for him. The one fighting his own cause, his reputation, his name, everything at stake as well as the reputation and future of the many who had joined him, fell upon Sobieski with the power of a thunderbolt and attacked him as soon as he emerged from the morass. Thus the royal army was overpowered before it could come into action, and the King, beholding the defeat of his army, from the first side, had only himself to blame for the useless destruction of four thousand of his own troops. Indeed, the whole army would have been destroyed had not Sobieski brought it off the field of action with the greatest skill under such difficulty. Though a defeated general is usually blamed, in this case every one attributed the loss of the day where it belonged — to the blunder of the King.

The King, now filled with regret at his foolhardiness in refusing to abide by the counsel of Sobieski, encamped upon the banks of the river Pilcza, where he showed a willingness to receive counsel and advice.

Lubormirski, far from feeling elation at his late victory, sought to make his peace with the King.

He was inflexible in no point save that which he deemed to be to the best interests of his army and his country, and, having secured satisfaction for them, he was content with having the decree of his proscription revoked and asked for no further favor for himself.

Being restored to kingly favor, Lubormirski disbanded his army and went to Jaroszin, accompanied only by his principal generals, where he met the King. The reconciliation was effected, but it was in such a way as it always is between a king and a subject who is himself dreaded. But, being well acquainted with kings, and although perfectly free to remain in Poland, Lubormirski returned to Breslau, where he died, very suddenly, some six months later. It was openly charged by his friends that his death could not be attributed to natural causes.

Sobieski had learned to conquer while serving under an able master, but from now on was prepared to more than surpass any teacher he had ever known. Hitherto he had lived, since his reëntry into Poland, in almost a continuous state of combat in which, being unmarried, he had often risked ending his life and his family line together. He was at this time arrived at the age of thirty-six and if the thoughts of love and companionship, home and children, had entered his mind, they must have been put aside, for the lust of war and conquest, in the name of his native country, had taken the place of such ties, so that we find him now, not only an eligible match, but one who, on account of his magnetism, form and carriage, must have stirred the heart of more than one girlish bosom.

CHAPTER III

AMONG the maids of honor whom the Queen had brought from France, little suspecting that one of them was a future queen, the Polish nobles took particular notice of one whom the Queen herself particularly honored. The name of this young woman was Mary Casimira de la Grange, daughter of Henry de la Grange and Francis de la Chatre who had been governess to Queen Louisa. Thus the young woman united two of the most ancient families of the province of Bery, distinguished for having produced several of the marshals of France.

Genry de la Grange was better known as the Marquis d'Arquien, Captain of the Guard to Philip of Orleans, the only brother of Louis XIV. Mary, the daughter, who followed the Queen of Poland, married Radziwil, palatine of Sendomir and Prince of Zamoski (a town of Poland in the palatinate of Beltz), and was the mother of four children who died very young and who were not long survived by the Prince.

Sobieski, persuaded that favor is a good support to merit, and knowing that the Queen continued her protection over the young widow, asked the hand of the Princess Mary in marriage so precipitately that she scarce had time to dry her tears from the demise of Prince Radziwil. In order to preserve the decency of mourning, the Queen of Poland arranged for a secret marriage between Sobieski and Mary Radziwil and then wrote to the Marquis d'Arquien asking for his consent.

The Marquis d'Arquien replied that it was a thing unheard of to marry again in a month after the death of the former husband; that, for his part, he was not dazzled by the fame of Sobieski and that, knowing that his daughter had derived but little happiness from her first marriage he had resolved upon settling her again in her native country and had hoped that the well known equity of Her Majesty would have permitted him the full possession of the authority parents hold over their children, by all the laws of God and man, but that the thing being done without his consent, which consent had seemed unnecessary, the respect he owed a great king prevented him giving his sentiments in full and that he should not forget the offense committed by his daughter, Madame Zamoski, as he termed her.

Men should learn to submit to the inevitable, particularly when the inevitable has already happened, with better grace, and we fancy that the Marquis must certainly have written in quite a different manner could he have foreseen that the marriage of his daughter to John Sobieski was to elevate her to a throne and be the means of loading him with wealth and honors.

Pope Innocent XII never forgot that he gave his benediction to the nuptial ceremony, while he was the Apostolic Nuncio in Poland, and testified, upon all occasions, a singular affection for the illustrious pair.

The Queen of Poland, friend of Madame Sobieski, died in 1667, but Sobieski was still high in favor with the King, and held the esteem of the entire nation, a condition which was not always to last. His rise was also promoted by events which occurred, with uncommon rapidity, in his favor. When Lubormirski took up arms against the King it left the vacancy, — in the Grand-Marshalship, which Sobieski filled in 1665. A year after that the death of Czarneski made him Petty General. He had now but one step farther to go to become one of the most considerable persons in the Republic. And that one step was taken when Grand General Potoski passed away (1667), and Sobieski was advanced to Grand General, resigning the office of Petty General to Demetrius Wiesnowieski, palatine of Beltz.

These two Generals, Petty and Grand, receive from the King a staff called Boulaf which is a short mace terminating at one end in a large head, either gilt or massive silver, and sometimes enriched with jewels. But in the army it is not the staff that indicates the general, but a long lance adorned at one end with a horse's tail, contrived so as to be seen at a great distance, either on the march, in time of action or when in camp. Each general has his tent, Petty General on one side and Grand General on the other side of the line, each with this ensign of office which is called Boutchouk.

The power of the Grand General was limited only by his own will, but besides the staff of Grand General, Sobieski possessed in addition the office and title of Grand Marshal and by this means held within his power both civil and military authority, a circumstance which at first caused great murmuring because both the spirit and the customs of the Republic directed that these two offices should always be kept separate, as their union conferred too formidable a power upon one man, but Sobieski, by his subsequent conduct, put a stop to all discontent.

At this time, as if to try again the ability of Sobieski, an army of eighty thousand Tartars appeared upon the frontiers of the Kingdom, and the Cossacks, always in a state of irritation and insubordination against their rulers, always rebellious, always ready at any and all times to strike a blow against Poland, were ready to join now with the Tartars in their aim at her destruction.

The army of Poland, at this time, numbered not

over twelve thousand, and the department was in so low a state financially that the Grand Treasurer declared that there was not sufficient moneys to pay the old troops much less money for new forces necessary to go against the Tartars and Cossacks. The King was wholly abandoned to despair and daily became more and more disgusted with the crown so that he no longer exerted himself to support the irksome demands of his high position, and, as is to be supposed, the evil grew more and more, so that a way out was most urgent. The Tartars, sustained by the Cossacks, advanced hourly and rapidly and great apprehension was felt from the Turks.

In general, the people expected nothing but ruin for the Republic, but not so Sobieski. He did not despair, but if ever he needed a second with whom to share the burdens and discuss ways and means it was now, with the gates on every side in danger from foes from without. Yet every thing and every one seemed, at this most critical juncture, to fail and to make matters still more serious, Wiesnowieski, Petty General, fell seriously ill so that the whole burden fell upon Sobieski who labored constantly and consistently to increase his little, and apparently wholly inadequate, army. Undaunted he began the march over the extensive territory and was supplied with fresh recruits as he went. He formed bases of supplies and magazines of provisions and ammunitions.

He not only emptied his own private purse, but he borrowed funds to re-supply the public treasury so that, finally, he marched with twenty thousand men toward the palatinate of Russia to meet a hundred thousand soldiers and to try and defeat them.

With so small a force it became necessary to resort to pitting the strength of his wit against the foe rather than to try to meet so great a force with so small an one. Sobieski therefore decided to detach some of his troops and, under competent generals, he sent them out to scour the country and to harass the enemy continually and incessantly, himself marching on toward the camp of the enemy and as though victory were already his, he wrote to his wife who had gone on a visit to her native country, France, that upon such and such a day he would, with twelve thousand men, shut himself up in a fortified camp before Podahieoz, a place that Doroscensko, the Cossack general, intended to besiege and upon that day, and from that place, he would march out upon the enemy and, in the end, would ruin the powerful adversary.

Such faith in one's ability was almost sufficient within itself to accomplish the purpose, but when France, that is, the Court of France, was thus informed by Madame Sobieski of her husband's daring plan, the Prince of Conde, who at that time was considered as one of the very greatest soldiers and strategists of Europe, declared the act to be sheer madness, and that there was not one single grain of possibility for its success.

In the meantime Sobieski had called together a council of his officers and laid the plan before them in the eloquent, persuasive manner in which he was wont to address his army and its leaders, but with no exception they all condemned the plan as entirely impracticable and freely prophesied destruction for Sobieski and his army. The result of the counsel was not long in being spread among the common soldiery, who became disheartened, and it became necessary for the Grand General to address them as he had done the others.

" I am determined," were the memorable words upon that occasion, " to make no change in my plan. The event will show whether it be well laid or not. As to what remains, I lay no restraint upon such as have not the courage to face a glorious death. Let them retire and die in flight by the sword of a Cossack or a Tartar. For myself I shall stay here with those brave soldiers who love their country. This crowd of robbers makes no impression upon my mind. I know that Heaven has often given victory to small numbers, when animated with valor and can you doubt but God will be for us against these infidels? " And all who were present looked at each other in shame and amazement and not one thought again of leaving camp.

The Tartars were free to march on and penetrate into the heart of Poland, but they chose, rather, to deprive the kingdom of its only resources by attacking this little army with all their forces and they were too well acquainted with the fame of Sobieski to care to leave him behind them.

Sobieski had already taken some prisoners whom he made use of to menace the Tartarian General at a time when he had everything to fear for himself and his own small force. "Go," said he to the prisoners as he dismissed them, "tell the Sultan Nuradin that I will treat him in the same manner he treated my brother. I will have head for head." The only answer that Nuradin gave was to hasten the attack.

The enemy poured in upon the camp from all sides and on all sides was warmly received, while the artillery kept playing briskly. At length a way was forced in a weak place, but the Poles, rushing thither, drove them back, sword in hand, beyond the entrenchments. The plain was soon covered with the bodies of the slain. The Poles' loss was four hundred, but the Tartar loss could not be more than estimated in a general way, as they, according to their ancient custom, carried their dead off the field of battle and burned them so that they might neither be counted nor stench to pollute the air with poison.

Battles are not, ordinarily, of many hours' duration, a popular belief being to the contrary. Some of the world's greatest decisive battles have been fought and won in half a dozen hours, some in even less time than that. While of course, as in some well known and authentic cases, they have lasted for several days, in this case the battle raged backward and forward, over and round about the besieged camp, for seventeen days and each moment was fought as hungrily by either side as though that moment were to decide the fate of each. On the part of the foe, whose superior numbers gave them great confidence, it was attack upon attack, while upon the part of the besieged it was advance upon advance. The last day of all was the most bloody. Sobieski had given orders that the outlying detachments which had been harassing and scourging in unexpected places, should return to the main army, by easy and (to the enemy) insensible approaches, as their presence was more needed within the lines than without, for it was becoming evident that the Tartars, provoked, disheartened and chagrined by such great resistance from so small a band, had resolved upon a general assault and that the moment was near at hand which would decide the fate of the Republic.

Sobieski realized, as did each and every man in the army, that if they were lost, Poland was lost;

that they and the Republic would then be at the mercy of Tartar and Cossack in whom was neither mercy nor the fear of God. This little Spartan band had learned from former experience that the troops of the opponent were not invincible, but the opponent, when it became a surety that they were to be met with at least a brave front, set up a cheer of derisive howling, but the joyful cries of the barbarians were almost instantly lost in the clamor of battle. A very deluge of blood was spilt and victory seemed wavering in the balance, but before either side could claim an advantage the several detachments arrived and attacked the enemy in flank. The brave Piwot, in particular, having laid in ruins the quarters of the Cossacks, carried off their convoys, defeated their foraging parties, redoubled his glorious efforts and attacked, sword in hand, with his two thousand cavalrymen, driving all before him. At the sight of such splendid fighting, in the face of such odds, the very sutlers and peasants converted everything they could find into weapons and resolved to do their part and to have a part in the victory which was by now but feebly disputed. The carnage would have been universal had not the victors been wearied with so much bloodshed.

The Tartars, little accustomed to pitched battles, began to look behind them and soon after gave way, lost their ranks, and became so utterly demoralized that confusion and dismay prevailed among them. When they saw that they had lost they took to flight and drew the Cossacks with them.

At this hour Sobieski, whose bravery and skill had animated the whole engagement, hoped to keep his word with Nuradin and ordered his life to be spared should he be overtaken on the route of flight, that he himself might have the grim pleasure of sacrificing him for the sake of avenging his brother's death. But Nuradin and Doroscensko had retired so early that they feared no pursuit, leaving behind them twenty thousand of their dead upon the field of battle. The full horror of the Tartar-Cossack ravages was revealed after the retreat of the enemy. The Poles saw with horror the sacked villages, the country seats and town palaces of the nobles as they lay razed to the ground, the churches smoldering in their ruins upon which lay great heaps of rotting carcasses and the frontiers entirely laid waste, but the body of the state was preserved and Sobieski's success not only astonished and electrified Poland but all the world joined in the acclaim to the great statesman-soldier who had accomplished the seemingly impossible. He had not only won a victory but that victory was over their most terrible foe and was a victory unparalleled in modern warfare. By this single achievement he had earned the right to be called the greatest soldier of his age and his glory is still undimmed by the Napoleons, the Washingtons or the Lees who have come after him. It was not only a victory as victories are estimated, but so great was the achievement that the foe was in utter panic and terror, an unheard of state for a Cossack or Tartar, who had begun the war but who now groveled for peace which the conquerors were more than glad to grant.

Sobieski now returned to the capital of Poland, victorious. He received the acclaim and plaudits of a grateful people all the way. Each village, each hamlet vied in doing him homage. He was, beyond peradventure, the savior of his people, of his country, and was received at the capital with every demonstration of joy, and right amid the shouts of the admiring multitude, he received news that filled him with greater joy than he had ever known. And that news was the message that unto him a son had been born, in Paris, where his wife was visiting, and where she had gone for her accouchement that she might be near her own people while her husband followed the uncertain fortunes of war. This child was afterwards known as Prince James. Louis XIV, the Grand Monarch of France, was his godfather. The child was named in full James Louis Sobieski, thus uniting the names of his illustrious grandfather and godfather.

CHAPTER IV

WINTER was the season allotted for the Diets, that the operations of war should not be interrupted. That of the present year was opened in the month of February. The Republic of Poland had many customs which resembled the customs of ancient Rome and which the student may apply as he will. The Grand General gave, as was customary, an account of the instructions he had received from the Senate, of the operations and success of the latest campaign, or the campaign which had been entered upon since the convening of the previous Diet, told of the distinguished actions of those who shared his labors, dwelling much longer upon the accounts of his co-laborers than upon his own deeds, and his address was received with applause by all the orders of the assembly whereupon the Vice-Chancellor, rising from his seat at the foot of the throne, gave solemn thanks, in the name of the Republic, to this deliverer of his country in her sore distress and to all who had assisted in the preservation of Poland. His remarks were but a degree less animated, all of which was a most worthy manner of receiving the returning heroes and one which few, if any, countries of Europe could have emulated, as in pure monarchies the King must receive all the attention, flattery and popular applause.

Casimir, King of Poland at this time, had nothing to do, no part to take in this great victory beyond ordering prayers over the success of the campaign and giving solemn thanks to God in the great church of Warsaw.

No doubt the occasion gave him more liberty to give vent to the deep religious trend of his nature, but, notwithstanding the victory of his army, a feeling of melancholy and despair was upon his spirits. He was inconsolable for the loss of his Queen, and yet by no uncommon contradiction between the judgment and the affections, his conscience was uneasy at having married her, she having been his brother's wife. Although the authority of the Pope had long since quieted his religious scruples, he now looked upon himself as accountable for all the calamities which the voice of the Republic had openly attributed to his marriage and his administration. His mind was so completely overwhelmed with grief that he became insensible to the burdens, the responsibilities of royalty, and soon after this surrendered the crown and retired to a monastery in France.

Upon the abdication of Casimir, several candidates presented themselves for the crown of Poland. The Czar of Muscovy's son, Ragotski; Prince of

Transylvania; the young Duke of Anguein; and in case of his rejection, the Prince of Conde, his father. There were also some others who entered the lists: Prince Charles of Lorraine — son of Duke Francis; and the Duke of Newberg, Palatine of the Rhine.

The Republic soon dismissed the first four for different reasons. The Czar's son on account of religion, though he offered to renounce that. Ragotski was rejected because Poland was still smoking from the fires of that war which his father had kindled in the kingdom, and the objections to the Duke of Anguein were his extreme youth and a certain crime which was committed by another, it having been in his favor that Casimir had attempted to bring the premature election which was against the most sacred precedent and law of the country. Even France had withdrawn from the young Duke her protection and had given it to his father, Prince of Conde. The son could only give promise of future merit while the father was already an accomplished statesman and soldier, renowned for the many battles in which he had been the victor, never having been conquered except by Turenne, which was a defeat but without in any way dimming his well deserved glory. It required the greatest of exertion and influence to blast the chances of such an one for the crown, but that blow was struck by no less a personage than Louis XIV himself, who had treated with the Swedes for the election of the Prince, but a sudden upheaval had changed the interests of France, the elector of Brandenburg having identified himself with his enemies and made himself formidable in the low countries. It was of great importance to disunite him from this ally and it was as a sop to him that the crown of Poland was presented to his view for the Duke of Newberg, from whom the Elector expected great advantages. Therefore Louis XIV hesitated not at all in making it known to the Poles that he desisted from his first demands and presented the Duke of Newberg for their consideration.

The situation, when the Diet was finally opened in the month of May, was acute. For, with the throne vacant, all the courts of justice and all, in fact, all governmental machinery, is at a standstill and all the power of authority was transferred to the Primate, who, in quality of interest, had more authority than even the King, but as he had no time in which to make a surplus of power a formidable weapon the Republic never objected to it.

Picture to yourself a great, free people going unto the Fields of Wola, at the gates of Warsaw, to choose their king. It must have been, indeed, an inspiring sight. All the nobles of the kingdom had the right of ballot. The Poles upon one side, the left side of the Vistula, the Lithuanians upon the opposite bank, each with its respective banner, and making a sort of civil army amounting to from one hundred to one hundred and fifty thousand men — even sometimes as high as two hundred thousand — assembled together to exercise the highest act of freedom, the right to vote.

In this great assemblage, those who were not able to provide themselves with horse and sabre stood behind, on foot, and armed with scythes which did not seem to make them feel one whit the less proud, as they had the same right of voting as the mounted, armed men.

Just here it may be well to explain that the title of nobility, in Poland, did not necessarily signify that the noble was a man of wealth or opulence. Sometimes quite the contrary, for a man was ennobled by the king for any conspicuous act of bravery or for any generous and noble deed. Possession of land, learning or heredity had nothing whatever to do with the creation of nobles. For instance, Sobieski, after his great victory at Vienna (which was in 1683 and is anticipating by about fifteen years), ennobled every man who was in his cavalry, but such a title of nobility could not extend to his progeny, still during life such nobles had all the powers and privileges of the hereditary noblemen, for they, too, were king makers, and not only could the entire nobility assist in making kings, but by inversing the law, they could unmake them as well, hence due provision was made, in cases of emergency or necessity, to remove a king with the slightest preliminary or ceremony.

In this election, on the field of Wola, all who openly aspired to the throne of Poland were expressly excluded from the field of election, that their presence might not embarrass or in any way whatsoever influence the voters.

The Polish king must be elected by a total suffrage, even one dissenting voice having the power to deprive him of the crown. As an instance worthy to recount, one noble opposed the election of Uladislus VII, and upon being asked what objection he could possibly find, he coolly replied, " I will not say. That is my own concern. I will not permit him to be king." The proclamation was, therefore, suspended for some hours and the interim devoted to making an effort to win over this noble who had chosen to block the election. It was finally accomplished and the king was most anxious to know upon what the noble had based such strong opposition. His reply was: " I was determined to see whether the rights of a single nobleman against the entire voice of the remaining nobility would be respected or whether it was an idle boast, and whether our liberty was still in existence. I am satisfied that it is and you can depend upon me, sire, as one of the most loyal subjects of the realm."

This law, strange as it may seem to us in an age when the will of the majority is decisive, was after all perhaps a wise one, at least it was quite plausible in theory, but had it been kept rigorously Poland could not have had such a thing as a lawfully elected king. They therefore gave up a real unanimity and contented themselves with the appearance of it; or rather, if the law which prescribed it could not be enforced that law was proscribed and if money could not sufficiently persuade the electors, then the assistance of the saber was sought. So ends in dust and ashes too finely wrought theories of government as the proper ending for all theories that will not bear the light of practical application.

However, before the Poles ever came to the extremity of arms to settle any election, their elections were carried on with enviable decorum and every appearance of freedom. The Primate, in a few words, recapitulated to the mounted Nobles, the merits of the candidates, setting forth, in detail, their lives, their characters, their achievements and their qualifications for the crown. He exhorted them to choose the most worthy; invoked Heaven, gave his blessing to the assembly and returned and remained alone with the marshal of the Diet while the Senators dispersed themselves into the several palatinates to promote a unanimity of sentiment. If the effort was successful, the Primate, himself, went to collect the votes, naming all the candidates, once more, and upon the name of their choice the nobles replied " Szoda," meaning " That is the man of our choice," and immediately the air resounded with his name with cries of " Vivat " and the noise of pistols. If all of the palatinates agreed upon one name then the Primate mounted on horseback and, amidst the most profound silence, succeeding the greatest noise, he asked, three successive times, if all were satisfied. Upon a general approbation, he three times proclaimed the King of Poland. The Grand Marshal of the Crown took up the proclamation and voiced it three times more at the three gates of every camp. Ah, how glorious a sovereign this, possessed of royal qualities! And how glorious his title to king when given by the suffrages of a whole nation.

This sketch of a free and peaceful election is not, we regret to say, what always occurred. The corruption of the great; the fury of the populace; intrigues and factions and, finally, the corrupting power of foreign gold, aye, and of arms too, sometimes filled the air with strife and bloodshed.

CHAPTER V

IN the year 1668 the assembly was already proceeding to vote and the decisive moment approached when Debiczski, standard bearer of Sendomir, a man venerable for his sanctity of manners and gray hairs, gave the Equestrian Order to understand that the faction of the Prince of Conde was reviving; " that he would be proclaimed at a time least expected if measures were not speedily taken to prevent." Immediately the Equestrian Order ran to the Senate and insisted upon excluding the Prince. The demand was most perplexing and the Primate sought his reply in the eyes of the Senators.

Sobieski, as Grand General, should have been upon the Frontier, but, as a possible aspirant, he was prohibited by the law from a seat in the assembly, but the high credit he had acquired by his personal power seemed to have raised him above the constitution, which is always indicative of weakness or decay in a republic where the laws should, at all times, be more respected than any great man, as the laws are (if not, they are supposed to be) the people's will, and in a pure republican form of government the will of the people should be the highest tribunal, else it is no longer a republic. But alas! In all of the world's history this is seldom the case. Sometimes a great name shorn of all former or accompanying honors has been the means of robbing a nation of its liberty. The election of Louis Napoleon as President of France is an apt illustration of this lamentable fact. At the time of his election to that high office, he had achieved nothing; his morals were bad; every effort he had made for fame had simply ended in notoriety. He was utterly wanting in genius, in character and in all of the great qualities of his great uncle, Napoleon Bonaparte. And yet, the splendors of the Emperor's name had so dazzled and hypnotized the French people that they had chosen him to be their leader on the very threshold of their freedom. Such a step was the cause, as is too well known to reiterate, of their downfall in three years.

Sobieski, observing the perplexity of the Primate, rose up to speak. It was to his interest that an exclusion should be pronounced against the Prince, for, although he was not a candidate, that is, his name had not been mentioned, so far, in connection with the crown, yet the natural intuition of so great a mind must have told him that the free nation might at any time look beyond the avowed candidates and that when it did it might be to himself, as its deliverer, that the eyes of the voters might look; that it was more than probable that the hero did flatter himself with this ambitious thought, there is no doubt, and yet this is the manner in which he spoke: " There is a wide difference in refusing to vote for the candidate and excluding him. A refusal is only an exercise of freedom; an exclusion is a direct affront. If the Equestrian Order proposes to restrain, in this manner, the liberty of the Senate, I will neither submit to such slavery nor have any share in affronting a great prince, but will quit the assembly. If the voters are contented with refusing him their suffrages it is well known that I will always yield to the voice of the electors." But the next day the demand to exclude the Prince became universal so that the Primate pronounced it against his own opinion and that of the Senate.

For a time, now, tranquillity was restored. The attention of the assembly was next directed toward the young Duke of Newberg and Prince Charles. Their virtues, their vices, the good and the evil that the Republic might expect from them if either was chosen, were discussed. It is at such a tribunal, where a Prince presents himself for trial, as it were, that a Prince may know exactly what may be thought or spoken of him, and Poland was unique in that respect at that day. Even in this progressive age, the Emperor of Germany and the Czar of Russia have not the slightest knowledge of the real sentiment of their subjects toward them, as all expression is most strictly prohibited and if by any oversight some bold spirit is allowed such expression his utterances and writings are quickly suppressed.

But, tempting as such philosophizing is, to proceed to the doings of the Diet, the Senate, the Deputies and nearly all of the Grandees who were for the Duke of Newberg, allowed the good qualities of the Prince of Lorraine, but, after having softened that of his rival, they boasted much of his possessions and of his wonderful promises to the Republic. A body of troops maintained at his own expense, a year's pay to the national forces, a military school for the young nobility, with a fund to assist them in traveling, were indeed advantages and promises that rolled well from the tongue, but Prince Charles was not in a condition to keep such promises as his fortune was not adequate, the French having but recently dispossessed his father of his dominions. " If we refuse *him*," added they, " we have no inconvenience to apprehend upon that account, but if we reject the Duke of Newberg let us reflect that the Powers which have proposed him have armies to make their wishes commands not to be disobeyed without due consideration."

Here we have the very first intimation, in the life of the Republic, not alone of the corrupting power of gold but of fear of foreign armed Powers. But when that fear was spoken, as it had just been, a sudden wrath was kindled that swept throughout the entire assemblage. The Senate, the Great Officers and the Deputies were ill defended by the entrenchments that surrounded the Szopa, which was then a vast building of wood, erected in the fields of Wola, for their reception. One part of the Republic besieged the other. Several discharges were made as a prelude to what might follow. The Senators and Deputies were seen throwing themselves from their seats, running here and there, or lying flat upon the ground while the balls whistled over their heads. Some arrived at the gates of the camp, but were received with a discharge of firearms at their breasts. Some were killed and a large number were wounded, and all forced to return to their places to preserve their lives. Every moment the tumult increased and Potozski, Marshal of the Diet, interposed to quiet it, but it was with great difficulty that they refrained from insulting him and the uproar continued. Nothing is harder to do than to keep voters, particularly voters for the filling of high offices, within bounds.

From the first opening of this more than notable Diet, hardly a night passed when persons were not assassinated on the streets of Warsaw or upon the field of election. Sobieski had, upon double authority, the right to exact obedience, for as Grand Marshal he was entrusted with civil authority and as

Grand General he had the army at his command and as soon as he exerted his authority he struck awe into the hearts of the people at Warsaw, for he threatened to send for troops and fire upon whatever party that might attempt to disturb or hinder the freedom of the election. The fear of his executing his threats suspended the rage of the assembly and order was once more restored and tranquillity reigned again over the field of Wola.

" To what purpose —" asked he, " are we murdering one another for Princes whom we have never seen, and in whom we have not the slightest interest and who, perhaps, in reality have no interest in Poland, but would make use of the power given them, no doubt, to smite us in return. Our fathers were far more wise. Scarce was the nation settled when it was divided, as we see it now, among a number of foreign candidates. The calamities which then threatened restored the use of reason. A native of Poland was chosen and this man, who had neither birth, nor prestige nor fortune, governed with such freedom and wisdom that to this day every Polish king is called Piast out of gratitude to that one. Let us leave the Duke of Newberg to govern his large family and small dominions. Let the Prince of Lorraine employ his money in recovering his hereditary territories. Let us imitate our forefathers and choose a Piast."

This is not the first instance in the world's history when a wise speech has calmed an excited and tumultuous crowd. But what Piast to choose was a difficulty not easily overcome. The assembly, as one man it seemed, turned its eyes upon Sobieski, but if at this point he had flattered himself that the crown was his for the taking, his illusion was of short duration. The more one reflects upon history, ancient or modern, the more he will believe that human affairs are the sport of fortune. The man whom she secretly destined for the throne of Poland at this time was one upon whom the public had given no thought. He, in fact, was so little interested in the election that he was not found in his tent, but in a convent at Warsaw and his name was Michael Wiesnowieski. The two palatines, Opalinski and one other, conducted him to the field of election, without informing him of their design, and there they proposed and nominated him. Olsowski, the Bishop of Culm and the Vice-Chancellor of Poland, cried out in an enthusiastic strain, " Long live King Michael." The cry flew, immediately, from mouth to mouth; all the orders repeated it and nothing was wanting but the Primate's proclamation. The Nobles forced him to it with a pistol at his breast and Wiesnowieski was King.

CHAPTER VI

THE man most surprised in the result of the election was Wiesnowieski himself. He wept as they dragged him to the throne and protested that he was incapable of filling it and the truth is that he was not, and a further truth is that since the Poles had rejected all foreign candidates and had determined upon choosing a Piast it would seem that they should not have hesitated for a moment between Wiesnowieski and Sobieski. Wiesnowieski was scarce thirty years of age; Sobieski, ten years his senior, had nearly reached that maturity of age which is so essential in the ruler of a country. Wiesnowieski's youth had been totally unemployed; Sobieski's had been spent in traveling, in the study of public business and in the fatigues, hardships and exposures of war. Wiesnowieski had held no office in the state; Sobieski had obtained the highest by acts of distinction and glory and still went on to acquire new victories, new glories, new honors, new triumphs. Wiesnowieski even lacked that importance which riches are supposed to confer. He was poor in purse, living, heretofore, upon a pension bestowed by Queen Louisa, and upon the liberality of the Bishop of Plocsko;

Sobieski had a vast estate, one of the largest in Poland and possessed a large number of vassals.
Wiesnowieski came to the election with the crowd
of Nobles to join his suffrage with theirs; Sobieski,
the first personage of the Republic, under the king,
seemed to present himself rather to receive the boon
at the hands of the assemblage than to assist in giving it to another man. One circumstance, only,
spoke in favor of the new King, and that was his
birth. He descended from Koribut, uncle of the
Great Jagellon; his father was Jeremiah Wiesnowieski, palatine of Russia and who, although having
been possessed of a vast estate in the Ukraine, had
been stripped of it by the Cossacks and thereby left
his son, Michael, almost penniless, with nothing more
than a distinguished name, however empty, but no
distinguished name, however worthy the ancestry,
was supposed to aspire to such high honors unless
fitted to fulfill the duties of the same.

Never was there a king who needed, nay wanted
perhaps, more to be governed than poor Michael
Wiesnowieski, and in this case, as in innumerable
others, a weakling has always a crafty, wily Mephisto
waiting to be called upon. The man ready and willing to get the government into his own hands was
Casimir Paz, Grand Chancellor of Lithuania, and
he possessed all of Michael's confidence.

Now Casimir Paz was not exactly unprincipled,

but he was possessed of an inordinate ambition which sometimes overweighed his love of country, and to which was bent his great abilities as a cultivated gentleman and superior orator, and withal selfish, he soon thought of promoting the interests of his own family rather than those of his country.

Sobieski, however, stood up once more in defense of Poland and prevented her from being despoiled and ravaged.

The Cossacks, notwithstanding the peace they had made with the Republic during the reign of Casimir, began to entertain grave suspicion as to the designs of the new king, Michael. They feared that he might have a mind to recover the possessions of his family in the Ukraine, as well as of the other Polish Nobility who had been robbed of their estates. To dispel these fears, the Cossacks demanded a renunciation of these claims, and the Poles, on their side, were most unwilling to begin a war at a time when the Kingdom was greatly exhausted. What was needed, at this critical period, was a diplomat who had the confidence and respect of the Cossacks as well as the implicit confidence of the King. There was only one person who seemed capable of filling the bill so far as both sides were concerned, but for reasons, which we shall soon show, the King did not desire to exalt that man to the high diplomatic post, although it was assumed to be but a temporary honor that would be required of any one.

Unfortunately for all, the young king had hardly been made the chief ruler when he began to grow jealous of the National Idol, for he knew that he was not only idolized, but that he was loved far more than he, the King, might ever hope to be, and the leader of the almost rebellious Cossacks, that same Doroscensko whom Sobieski had already beaten, was inflexible. It became necessary, so deemed the King, to have recourse to arms, that last resource of Kings which has spilt so much blood, needlessly, ever since the time when men first began to put up masters over their heads. Sobieski, warrior that he was, shed as little as possible for he rightly considered the blood of the Cossacks as belonging to the Republic, since they had really been good subjects before the Poles had made bad slaves of them. It has been so hard for conquering nations to believe that more is gained, after conquest of arms, by kind, humane and just treatment than by imposing double burdens upon the conquered who are already smarting under the sting of the lash of learning to subjcet themselves to new rulers and, perhaps, also, strange customs. Another cause for the mild treatment which Sobieski accorded the Cossacks was that his own troops were so depleted that he had recourse to artfully sowing divisons among the Cossacks themselves. He set up new leader against old; Hanensko against Doroscensko. He reduced to the obedience of Poland the cities of Bar, Nimirow, Kalnic and Braslaw and all the country between the Bog and the Niester. Doroscensko having been entirely overpowered, had no way of saving the balance of the Ukraine but by threatening to give it over to the Turks, if he was driven to extremities, and this threat made Sobieski suspend operations.

The congratulations that Sobieski received showed plainly the importance of the campaign. "We cannot sufficiently admire your valor and prudence in this expedition. With such a handful of men how could you recover so many towns and cities, and particularly Braclaw, which alone is a worthy victory. You have opened to us a passage into the Ukraine and will, doubtless, complete its destruction. Even envy itself is forced to own that Poland is indebted to you for its safety." These are the terms in which the Vice-Chancellor wrote Sobieski in the name of the King and the entire Republic, and in this manner the Grand General took his revenge for having missed the crown. And what a noble revenge it was. How few examples we have of such sublime self renunciation, which was anything but renunciation, for, was not he steadily gaining and growing in the love of an already worshipful and grateful people? It is no wonder that he was destined to write his name so high, not only as a soldier, but as the wisest and best of conquerors and Kings.

However, Sobieski insisted that, without abusing the privileges of victory, to which belongs the spoils, the Poles should treat the Cossacks with kindness and consideration so that, eventually, they might look upon their subjection as a blessing. He sought to bring them back to allegiance by clemency, and the alluring hopes of future prosperity. Had this advice of Sobieski been followed, how much blood and treasure might have been spared, and in after years Poland would not have had fall upon her such evil days.

This idea of treating the Cossacks with clemency was also the opinion of the Deputies and of the greater portion of the Diet, but the King and his council thought differently.

The reign of Michael was the reign of favorites, as is the reign of every weakling, and his Council was made up of pensioners to the Emperor Leopold, the Austrian, whose sister Michael had lately married. And as Leopold was apprehensive of a formidable invasion which was then preparing in Turkey, he had devised a plan which was likely to divert it upon Poland. He therefore had no difficulty in pursuading the Polish monarch that all negotiations with the rebel Cossacks were no less dangerous than mean and beneath the dignity of his high and commanding position. He also had no difficulty in making Michael believe that to pardon Doroscensko was to weaken the royal authority. Michael thought himself great by showing himself a weak tool in the hands of the crafty Austrian.

Doroscensko, by some means, was soon made aware of the attitude of the King, and, fearing to fall into the hands of a provoked sovereign, he went to Constantinople to make terms with the Turkish ruler.

The conditions in Turkey were, briefly, these: Mahomet IV, on his way to the throne, had passed over the body of his father, Ibrahim I, whom the janizaries had strangled. He had never yet appeared in person at the head of his armies, but his successes seemed unalterable under the management of the Grand-Vizier, Cuprogli, a man of abilities equally exalted with his station. The Turks who never gave place to sentiment made exception for Cuprogli, and termed him "The Light of Nations," "The Guardian of the Laws," "The Formidable Commander."

The saying of Montecuculi, upon retiring from public life, when his rivals finished their course is well known, and also serves as the best possible definition of the standing of Cuprogli. "Should a man who has had the honor of fighting with Turenne, Conde and Cuprogli hazard his glory against persons who are only beginning to command armies?" but that was as regards the military character of

Cuprogli which was all that Montecuculi had any knowledge of.

Cuprogli reflected upon the offer which Doroscensko made in which it was designed to conquer Poland, deferring until another campaign the destruction of the Empire of Vienna, as a victory which would be facilitated by the conquest of Poland.

Hereupon a manifesto was immediately addressed to Poland, and it was necessary, without delay, to fix upon some expedient for saving the Republic. In the Senate, Sobieski spoke with great warmth upon the advisability of appeasing the Cossacks and pointed out the articles in which Poland might make concession, but there is no such thing as persuading weak minds, much less princes who are accustomed to no distinction between might and right. Michael persisted in his obstinacy and returned the Porte no answer as if the menaces were of no consequence.

From this period may be dated the inception of the league which was formed to dethrone Michael. It is a maxim — we repeat — with the Poles that whatever people has the right to make its king has also the right to unmake him. So that what, in other countries might be called a conspiracy was merely looked upon as a national privilege. Among the chiefs of this league were the Primates, Prazmowski, Sienawski, the Great Standard Bearer, Lubormirski, Palatine of Cracow, Ledchinski, of Masovia, Potoski, of Kiovia, Vielopolski and other nobles of equal importance. The enterprise was nothing like as hazardous as it would have been in hereditary kingdoms, but yet it had its dangers.

The confederated nobles thought it proper to show their regard to the Emperor Leopold by acquainting him with their designs particularly on account of his sister who shared the Polish throne with Michael. They therefore laid before Leopold all the grievances of the state and poor Michael's incapacity to govern.

In proud and haughty nations a lawful king who is despised totters upon his throne while usurpers who are esteemed sit firmly. The English never thought of deposing Cromwell; for Cromwell had humbled Holland, prescribed the conditions of a treaty with Portugal, beaten the Spaniards, forced France to court his alliance and given the empire of the seas and of commerce to England: France never thought of deposing Napoleon for Napoleon had carried the eagle of France triumphant into every capital of continental Europe. He had made the name of France both glorious and one to be feared by his wonderful achievements, but as for Michael — he was fit for nothing but to ruin Poland.

CHAPTER VII

HITHERTO the Confederated Nobles, uncertain of Sobieski, whose conduct seemed to indicate an unwillingness to break with the Court, had communicated nothing to him of their design, but, having reflected upon the necessity of gaining him over, they now laid their plan before him. The part that Sobieski should take either for or against this would, in all probability, decide the fate of the King or the kingdom. With all the weight of his dignities as Grand General and Grand Marshal, and at the head of an army which thought itself invincible when headed by him, he espoused the cause of the kingdom against its weak and misguided King. But whether Sobieski, when he decided upon the deposition of Michael, aimed at fixing the attention of the nation upon himself, or whether he had nothing in view but the public good, it is certain that he represented to the Nobles just how dangerous it would be to take Leopold's nomination of a king and, in conformity with the love he always bore France, he proposed the Duke of Longueville whose only merit lay in valor which, alone, will never make a great ruler. The Confederacy was too anxious for a change and to overthrow the present incumbent to weigh things as carefully as they might have done, and trusted implicitly and acquiesced to the proposal. They made the utmost expedition to make their wants known to France and the thing was done with so much secrecy by Sobieski that neither the Court of Vienna nor the Court at Warsaw had the slightest suspicions as to what was going on.

The abrupt dissolution of the last Diet, the one in 1672, furnished the conspirators with a well grounded pretext of calling another, and the King dared not refuse, more especially as it was become necessary to put the Republic in arms, as it was learned that the Turks were actually upon the march.

Never was a king treated in so unbecoming a manner before his subjects. The Primate, taking advantage of the ferment, addressed Michael in terms such as would have been, in an absolute monarchy, nothing short of high treason, and while he was still speaking, the Nobles, whose number was greatly increased in the national assembly, signified to Michael that it was the desire that he should voluntarily abdicate at once and that if he failed to do this he would be forced to at the point of the bayonet.

As soon as Michael saw that Sobieski was in the league against him he despaired of holding the crown and the catastrophe daily approached nearer and nearer. The splendid equipages advanced toward the sea coast in order to receive the Duke of Longueville, whom they destined for the crown, but that Prince was still upon the banks of the Rhine, which Louis XIV was attempting to pass, and where every one knows that the Duke met his death by wantonly firing a pistol upon some Dutchmen who begged their lives upon their knees. " Those scoundrels " (to make use of his own expression), to whom he ordered the French to give no quarter, gave him none. Thereby the Duke of Longueville realized the truth of the saying of Jesus —" As you mete it out to others so shall it be meted unto you." And with his death was ended the branch of Orleans-Longueville. The death of the Duke utterly disconcerted the League and gave renewed hope to Michael.

The King, somewhat uncertain as to whether he was still King or no, assembled all the nobility of the lower order, amounting to several hundred thousand men, in the field of Golemba, upon the banks of the Vistula, in the palatinate of Lublin. He had formerly been one of their body and lived upon a level with them, and to them he was, principally, indebted for the scepter. By them he was beloved as an equal and respected as a king. He chose Steven Czarneski for Marshal of the Royal Confederacy, with power to raise a new army and restore the ancient militia, called Hastata on account of the lance with which it was armed.

Poland acknowledged but two grand generals, but the action of the King in creating Czarneski a grand general made the third, and indeed a great deal more than the ordinary grand general was he, for, being armed with the thunder of war, *and* the sword of justice, he was, to all intents and purposes, a dictator who could acquit or condemn at pleasure. The Royal Confederates took an oath to maintain Michael upon the throne at the hazard of their lives and fortunes, and the sacredness of an oath was as much respected in the seventeenth century in Poland as it had been with their ancestors, the Samartians.

The Senators and all persons holding office were summoned to join the Royal Confederacy within a limited time, upon the pain of confiscation of their goods and loss of dignity if they failed to do so. The time allowed was very short, and had it not been for the stern resolution of Sobieski they must all have thrown themselves at the feet of their provoked monarch and his right hand, the dictator, and begged for mercy and clemency, but Sobieski knew too well that neither would be shown and that their only safety lay in pursuing the opposition.

The Grand Marshal, Sobieski, assembled the army, which now formed a most formidable confederacy,

opposed oath to oath, in the name of God and Sobieski, to maintain the rights and privileges of the
nation as delivered down to them from those ancient warriors who had sealed them with their blood.

Whilst the Republic was thus arming itself for
civil war, Mohammed advanced, like an angry sea, to
overwhelm Poland. The King, instead of going to
meet the Turks with the hundred thousand Nobles
which supported his tottering throne and showing
by such conduct that he deserved to reign, was employed in prosecuting the first subjects of his kingdom with all the severity of the law. Confiscation
of goods, loss of honors and dignities, degradation
from the ranks of nobility was decreed against all;
but against the leaders of the League, was pronounced, in addition, a sentence of death. Of the
latter class was Sobieski and the Primates and, to
complete the whole, a price was set upon their heads.

At this news the soldiery gave a shout of indignation against the King and the Confederated
Nobles; then, laying their sabers in the form of
crosses, swore to avenge and defend their General.

It was necessary that such a man as Sobieski had
become should, in the very nature of the struggle,
either perish or become the first man in the Kingdom. " I accept your protestations," he said, " but
first let us defend our country."

Sobieski foresaw that Mohammed would open a

campaign with the siege of Kamieniec, capital of Podolia, a place still stronger by nature than by art. It had been in all the centuries the bulwark of Poland against the Turks and the Tartars. Sobieski sent thither eight regiments of infantry to reënforce the garrison, but the Governor, who was wholly devoted to the King, was afraid that these troops would give Sobieski too great authority in the place and therefore refused to admit them, a fatal effect of the civil dissension.

To make matters worse, Mohammed appeared before Kamieniec with a hundred and fifty thousand men about the end of July. In addition, a hundred thousand Tartars arrived there, by his direction, at the same time so that his army totalled two hundred and fifty thousand, commanded upon this occasion by Cham-Selim-Geirai in person. For a long time the nation had had no such distinguished a commanding officer, nor such an able leader both in war and peace. The Turkish generals paid great heed to his judgment, and, with him at the head, the Tartars would undertake anything. In another country he would have introduced politeness, letters and arts, for whenever he could lay aside the saber he took up the pen, and Cantemir calls him an excellent philosopher and historian.

Cham-Selim Geirai had for lieutenant-generals his two sons, Sultan Galga and Sultan Nuradin.

Scarce had they paid their respects to the Grand-Siegnior than he ordered them to make incursions as far as the Vistula while the Cossacks, stimulated by resentment, carried desolation on another side. Mohammed was the idol of this great multitude which exhausted the earth but Cuprogli was its soul.

Sobieski, with thirty-five thousand troops, could not give battle to the Turks, before Kamieniec, with their overwhelming forces. He, therefore, abandoned this fortress to its horrible fate, for it was of the utmost importance to stem the stream of Tartars which was making its way toward the very heart of the Kingdom.

We must not lose sight of the hundred thousand soldiers under the King at Golemba, and Sobieski with his small troops at Lovicz. An imprudent step of Nuradin discovered to the Turks upon which side lay true courage and regard for the welfare of Poland. The young Tartar, as he coasted the palatinate of Lubin, took his course between the two armies in camps two. The King and his generals took it into their heads that this movement was planned in concert with Sobieski and the alarm felt was so great that the King did not feel himself safe surrounded with a hundred thousand armed Nobles, but took refuge within the walls of Lubin, a town about six leagues distant from where he was encamped, and the Nobles dispersed.

Sobieski, having nothing further to fear from his own countrymen, displayed all his greatness. The man who had just been condemned to death did his utmost to save his judges. He went in search of the Tartars wherever they appeared. His first victim was Nuradin, whom he overtook and defeated at the gates of Krasnabrod, a village in the palatinate of Lublin. The victory was so complete that the General escaped almost alone to the army of his brother, Sultan Galga, who, to avoid a like disaster, marched towards the Niester, in order to join forces with the Cham, but he was prevented by the amazing diligence of Sobieski and his loss exceeded that of his brother. The plain of Nimirow was covered with Tartars, breathing their last upon the booty they had carried away.

Sobieski, leaving his infantry with the baggage, followed the fleeing army with his cavalry.

Another battle was fought at Grudec and another at Komarna, whence the two sultans had escaped again in the utmost disorder. Having passed the Niester, they expected to have some respite with the shattered remnant of their forces, but Sobieski was tireless in their pursuit; they then threw themselves across two other rivers, the Stry and the Chevitz, which Sobieski also passed. At length the two sultans joined their father.

The Cham, who had as yet been in no engagement, was strong enough to avenge his two sons, but, being intimidated by their disasters, and still more solicitous over his vast plunder, its safety and preservation, which, however, embarrassed his army, rendering it that much less fit for service on the field, he sought only to avoid an engagement. This plunder, being the spoils, interested Sobieski still more than it did the Tartar, for, besides furs, silver and gold, the Tartars were carrying off vast herds of cattle, both for war and agriculture, and thirty thousand slaves of all ages, sex and conditions, most of whom were usually employed in tillage. The least valuable portion of the spoil was a number of monks.

The Cham kept fleeing but Sobieski never lost sight of him for a single hour, and, having more experience than the Tartars, waited for an opportunity to attack him with advantage. He found it, at last, at Kallusa, at the foot of the Crapec mountains, in a narrow pass where the enemy had not room to draw up their troops. The battle was very fierce and bloody for the Cham left upon the field some fifteen thousand of his troops and all of his booty. It was an affecting, and no doubt a most gratifying, sight to the patriotic Sobieski when the irons were taken from the thirty thousand Poles and put upon the Tartars who were taken after the action.

The multitude of unhappy wretches whom Sobieski had recovered had given up all hope of ever seeing home, wife and kindred, but now, filled with
gratitude for their deliverance, they fell prostrate
before their deliverer who, himself, fell prostrate before the God of battle.

CHAPTER VIII

POLAND was now delivered from the Tartars but not from the Turks. But if the hundred thousand nobles had attacked the Turks while Sobieski pressed upon the Tartars who knows if Kamieniec might not have been saved?

The Turks were perfectly acquainted with sieges before the Christians. At that of Candy they made parallel lines in their trenches. Upon the present occasion Cuprogli applied all his knowledge of the military art. For nearly a month an enormous train of artillery had been playing upon the place so that nothing was left but a heap of ruins and the rocks upon which they stood. This rock, however, was accessible only by means of a bridge, and the Vizier shuddered when he considered the Mussulman blood that must be shed, in an assault upon Kamieniec. He, therefore, took advantage of the Governor's blunder. He knew, as it was his business to know such things, that when the Governor had refused admittance to Sobieski and his soldiery he had admitted all the nobility of Podolia, men, women and children, who made his position more precarious than it might otherwise have been. The Vizier had recourse to bombs which, falling into such a small area which was overcrowded, heaped the dead upon the dying. The cries of the women and children enervated the soldiers and slackened the vigor of the defense, but there was no talk of surrendering. Cuprogli next employed another means of inflicting torture and terror. He gave the besieged to understand that if the place was not surrendered within twenty-four hours that all should be put to the sword, old and young, down to the very infant at the breast. This menace, accompanied by every indication of preparation for a general storm, struck terror into every heart and a parley was arranged and held on the 29th of August.

A major of artillery, enraged at the surrender of a place which might have been better defended, resolved not to survive so great a loss. At the entrance to the bridge there was a large tower that served for a powder magazine. In this he placed a match and mounted the platform from where he saw the Turks enter the place and the Poles run out to implore mercy of the besiegers. The magazine soon blew up and buried the officer who had fired it, with all else who were within a certain distance, both Turks and Poles, in the burning ruins. The deed was indeed a brave one, but the Poles who escaped had great difficulty obtaining a pardon for the crime of which they were not only innocent but ignorant.

Mohammed was now master of Kamieniec and Podolia. He sent garrisons into all the places of the Ukraine which was possessed by the Cossacks. The Poles, or rather that faction of Poland, which had oppressed the Cossacks repented, but the repentance was too tardy to undo the mischief still to be done by the Cossacks. Misfortune did not, however, end with this move upon the part of the Turkish generals, for, elated at so much victory, the Sultan resolved to push his armies into the very heart of the Kingdom. Each day but added its new disaster to the previous day's toll.

Sobieski brought back his victorious troops from the foot of the Crapac mountains, which divide Poland from Moldavia, Transylvania and Hungary. At this juncture if he had decided to get himself proclaimed King he would, probably, have succeeded, but he was wholly taken up with contriving how best to attack them so that his forces might have some chance of winning in the unequal contest.

King Michael was now in such a situation that he dreaded the success of his own General quite as much as that of the Turks, so he sent emissaries to Mohammed, encamped at Bouchaz, to sue for peace, offering to let him make all the conditions except one, keeping him, Michael, upon the throne, and this was

not at all disagreeable to the Sultan, for at that time
Podolia and the Ukraine were both flourishing provinces and both yielded to the conqueror, which was
Poland's material loss. Her utter abasement came
in the clause which engaged to pay an annual and
perpetual tribute to Turkey of a hundred thousand
golden ducats. One must be a Pole to conceive
just how humiliating and terrible was this dis-
graceful treaty which provided not alone for the loss
of two of its most powerful provinces, but for tribute
to the *despised Turks,* by a strong and powerful Republic which was, virtually, acknowledgment that
the Turks had at last conquered Her, so proud of
Her power and independence, now to bend to such a
galling yoke. And to climax the catastrophe, Her
King, like other lesser Princes, was glad to bend the
knee and become one of the first slaves of the Porte,
obliged to march at his command, against all the
enemies of the Ottoman Empire, Christians as well
as others. Such was the famous, infamous treaty
of Bouchaz.

The peace which Michael had just signed, not only
covered Poland with ignominy, but was an open vio-
lation of its laws and an affront to the whole people
which could not be borne. For a king of Poland
could make neither peace nor war without the consent of his subjects, and of all laws which have ever
been devised by the wisest of law makers, there is

none wiser.

Sobieski, whose hands were tied by the terms of peace, returned to his camp at Loviez. Michael, endeavoring to make a show of generosity and dignity without being possessed of either, sent an order to the army and to the Grand General, by name, to take a new oath of allegiance to him upon which condition he promised to forget the past and to restore all the proscribed to their former honors and estates. Sobieski replied that he and the army would take the required oath, provided that the King would make a new one for himself toward the Republic, without any equivocation, and swear to observe the articles which had been omitted from the Pacta Coventa by a designed precipitation. These articles were a security against all the violations over which the Primate had reproached him.

Michael was highly incensed at being put upon a level with the nation, as if it were an affront to that majesty which the nation alone could and had conferred upon him, and, provoked at the refusal of the proffered pardon, breathed nothing but vengeance.

However, in the present situation, there was much greater need that Sobieski should be pacified than the King. And Sobieski, armed and backed by a powerful faction, the King found it necessary, or rather expedient, to erase his name and all of the members of the League from the writs of proscription; after which he sent a deputation to the camp at Loviez to assure them of his affection and to invite them to a diet of pacification — which was held at Warsaw, February, 1673.

Whether it would be prudent for Sobieski to attend a diet of pacification was a subject of much conjecture in the army. The officers and soldiers represented, with great emotion, the dangers that might attend his acceptance, but heroes depend for protection upon their superior talents and majestic virtues rather than the ability to bow to the conventional.

Once in convention, it would seem that Sobieski, if any person present, had a right to assume a high and lordly manner on account of his triumph over the Tartars and his almost certain victory over the Turks but for the treachery of the King, but he forgot that there had been intended a scaffold for him and a price set upon his head. Upon these subjects no complaint escaped him. It was as though it had never been, but he painted, in the most glowing colors, the grievances of his country. The King was present to hear Sobieski, as his station obliged him to be in all assemblies of the Nation, but the preferment of the throne was awed by the genius of Sobieski. And Michael felt, in his poor, weak way that he was in the presence of his master and one destined to become great by the force of character. He had also another wound to bear, for Sobieski shed tears over the treaty of Bouchaz and appealed from the King to the Republic which had not yet signed away its rights for the life of slavery and ruin under the hated yoke.

Even under the fire of Sobieski's eloquence, it was affirmed and asked —" Such a proceeding is easy enough in Warsaw, but how will it be received in Constantinople? "—" With extreme indignation no doubt," was Sobieski's rejoinder to the query — " but we have courage and sabers still left us. We shall not wait for the enemy to come to us but must go to them instantly."

Dignity and eloquence, combined with virtue and sincerity, will always, had always, prevailed with great assemblies. The fire of the Polish Demosthenes caught the Senate and the Equestrian Order. The treaty of Bouchaz was declared void. Peace was broken and war begun. In fancy the Poles saw, already, the exalted Mohammed trembling under the sword of their Grand General.

In their commendations, the Poles have something of the swelling style of the Atlantic. Some declared that the Greeks would have taken Sobieski for the god Apollo, whose oracles disclosed futurity; others, were for revivifying the doctrine of Pythagoras and insisted that all the souls of all the great ancients were combined and had passed into the body of Sobieski. But one thing is certain and that is that

Sobieski was greater than the King who was compolled to listen to all this superlative praise from the lofty eminence of his throne.

CHAPTER IX

WAR having been decided upon and while the recruits were being raised and collected, Sobieski dispatched spies into Wallachia and Tartary towards the Danube and to the Turkish camp at Choczin; of which last they gave a terrifying account, describing it as looking like an immense fortress erected to command Poland on account of the communication it had, by means of bridges over the Niester, with Podolia and Kamieniec.

Sobieski was far from deceiving himself as to the risk he ran, but he was so pleased with the great project in view that he dispatched courier after courier to the Grand-General of Lithuania, Michael Paz, to hasten the march of his troops.

The Lithuanian troops failed to arrive before September was almost finished but finally came upon the plains of Glinian, a few leagues from Leopol, where the Poles impatiently awaited them, and their impatience was not without reason for it was high time the campaign were being closed rather than begun. The army, however, being at last assembled, advanced into the Bucovine, a forest thirty leagues long by as many broad, where a branch of the Crapac mountains forms defiles so extremely difficult to pass that a seasoned traveler can scarce do so without shuddering.

It seems probable that there was nothing known at Constantinople as yet regarding the advance of the Polish armies nor the breach of the treaty which such a march meant, for they were met by the Turkish envoy who was coming into Poland for the pur-' pose of collecting the first payment of the tribute agreed upon in the shameful treaty which Sobieski was determined to invalidate. The envoy behaved with all the haughtiness which he deemed his position as the envoy from a conquering to a conquered nation demanded and Sobieski respected the law of nations, allowing him to continue his journey unmolested while his army advanced into the forest where, it was expected, the passes would be disputed, but the enemy did not appear until they arrived upon the plain at the farther side and then there but a few bodies which retired with great rapidity.

Sobieski hastened his march along the banks of the Pruth and, leaving it, appeared on the ninth of November before the camp of Choczin. The town on the right side of the river was defended by a citadel and a fort on the left side covered the head of a bridge. It was in this very place, some fifty years previously, where Sobieski's father had performed such great achievements. The son was now attempting greater, with this difference only, that at that time the Poles defended the camp, and at the present they had come to attack it. The Seraskier Husseim, a disciple of the famous Cuprogli, was Commander in Chief, and had with him eighty thousand of those veteran troops that had conquered the isle of Candy.

A council of war was held in the night, in which Paz, weighing the inequality of forces, protested that it would be a punishable piece of temerity to expose to certain destruction the last hope of the Polish Republic, and that, as for himself, he would retire at sunrise with his Lithuanians, to preserve them for the service of his country.

Sobieski, more harassed by friends than enemies, answered that he had foreseen everything that now presented itself, except this resolution of Paz; that the situation of things was far from giving him any terror; that it was much more dangerous to retire before an enemy of superior strength, than to attack them; and that, in short, the only favor he desired of him was to stay and be a spectator of the first blows. What an appeal this was! Of a patient, supreme patriot, confident of his own power, and begging that those who should have been at his side, should at least witness his action when he should deal the first blow at their powerful enemy.

Paz himself loved glory, and since Sobieski was

obstinately bent upon seeking it, he would have been greatly mortified at his finding it without him.

On the 10th, everything was prepared for the attack. There was, in the Polish army, a body of Cossacks, gained over by Sobieski's liberality; their leader, Samuel Motovildo, impatient to signalize himself at their head, opened the scene, without waiting for the General's order.

But this day was not the day that Sobieski destined for the effusion of blood. He continued with his army in battalia, hoping that the enemy, with such a superiority, would come out of camp; but the day was spent in cannonading. Towards the evening, an unexpected event increased the forces of the Poles: On the right side of the Turks, there was a separate camp of between seven and eight thousand Walachian and Moldavian cavalrymen which, though Christians, were under the command of the Infidels. This was a source of great mortification and sorrow to the Christian heart of Sobieski. This war, after all, was nothing more nor less than a struggle between the contending faiths of the followers of Mohammed and the followers of Jesus, and now in this extreme hour, that a large and important force of Christians should be found ready to deal blows at the Christian army in behalf of the power of Mohammed was almost unthinkable. These troops did not answer the expectations of the Seraskier, either in number or beauty, and the two Hospodars who conducted them were therefore treated like slaves, showing the contempt which the followers of Mohammed always did show to such Christians, so called, when they found them ready to betray their country and their religion. The Seraskier even forgot himself so far as to strike the Moldavian with his battle-ax, with the result that the Princes, stimulated by lust for revenge, came and offered Sobieski themselves and their troops. The Turks beheld this desertion with indignation, but were unable to prevent it, and, whether or not Sobieski felt their offer a lofty one, it nevertheless was preferable to having them arrayed against him, if for no other reason than that of principle.

The following night was extremely severe for the soldiers to continue under arms. They were half frozen by the snow, which fell in great abundance, but when they saw Sobieski visit the posts, rest himself upon the carriage of a cannon and refuse a tent, they were encouraged. At break of day he observed that the enemy's ranks were thinner than usual; the same number of colors were flying upon the parapet, but much fewer janizaries were to be seen. The Turks, accustomed to a mildness of climate, which the Poles were unacquainted with, were less capable of fatigue. Their strength was exhausted by having been four-and-twenty hours under arms in such severe weather; and, thinking that the Poles would not dare to attack them in open daylight, they retired to take a little rest.

"This is the moment that I have waited for," said Sobieski, to the officers who were about him, "carry my orders for the attack," and he instantly set them an example, which, upon any other occasion would be found fault with in a general. Observing that the first brigades were wavering between courage and fear, he made his own regiment of dragoons, a troop formed by himself, alight from their horses; and, putting himself at their head, he marched up to the Turkish intrenchments. He was too bulky to mount with ease, and while his men were assisting him, he was all the while exposed to the enemy's fire, but at length appeared upon the parapet with his dragoons. The infantry, seeing his danger, and fearing for him, rushed on violently on the right and left to sustain him and, forcing the first posts one upon another, turned their own cannon against them.

In the meantime Jablonowski, Palatine of Russia, made a motion of the utmost importance. The cavalry had not yet forced its way, and the infantry was afraid of being surrounded if it advanced too far; he therefore came around by the camp which the Moldavians had quitted, and forced through with the Pancerns. Sobieski had fought on foot for near an hour; he was at length supplied with a horse, and the rest of the cavalry soon entered through the intrenchment itself.

Surprise occasions greater confusion than fire and sword. The Turks, being hard pushed on all sides, left many men and much ground; but the Poles, finding a greater number of empty tents than of enemies, stopped to pillage: a common fault with troops that are not under the strictest discipline, and a grave fault too. Many battles that are supposed to have been won have been lost again by the greed of the soldiers for plunder. If the victory was at all uncertain, it was at this juncture. The Turks, charmed at the power of their wealth, took courage and repulsed the victors. Sobieski, with the Towarisz, sustained this first shock, and was seconded by Jablonowski with Pancerns. Lesczinski, Palatine of Pudalchia, brought up the plunderers to their colors, and victory, which seemed to depart, appeared again, accompanied with order.

Sobieski, in the heat of action, did not neglect to take care of consequences. He ordered Baron de Boham, a French officer, to march to the bridge to cut off the enemy's retreat. By this time there were none who stood their ground, but the janizaries only, who dared not give way in the presence of the brave Solyman who commanded them. The Seraskier, on his part, did all that could be expected from a general who was forced in his camp. He recalled and brought back to action his broken squadrons.

But when some of the runaways, being repulsed from the bridge, brought intelligence that the retreat was cut off, the Turks, instead of deriving fresh courage from despair, had no sensation left, but that of terror. A body of between six and seven thousand cavalrymen endeavored to escape in a place where the rocks were lower than usual; but were charged by the Lithuanians, who forced their way by that very entrance, and drove them back upon the field of battle where they ran with full speed against a body of Polish cavalry. Sobieski, who was seen everywhere, and seemed to be at every place, happened to be in this body. Woe be to that General who, on such occasion, cannot act the soldier. Sobieski could and fortune assisted him as much as his own valor. A Turk aimed at him a mortal blow which was received by a young hero named Zelinski, whose death was quickly avenged; and there succeeded a series of single combats in the midst of a general action. At last, the Palatine of Kalisch and the Castlellan of Posnania came up with a body of horse, and disengaged the Poles. The whole camp was covered with dying infidels. The Spahis pursued on their horses at random, with no other view but to avoid the sabers of their pursuers. The Seraskier, covered with wounds, thought only how to save the ruins of his wretched army; but how to effect it was the difficulty. The only way of retiring that he could discover, was either over a few paths across the rocks, or upon the waves of the Niester.

From this moment the state of the Turkish army no longer presented the idea of a battle, but of a complete rout, where destruction was multiplied in all its various forms. Here the flying squadrons threw themselves from the top of rocks and were dashed in pieces against other rocks below, where men and horses were heaped one upon another; there the broken infantry took refuge towards the citadel, which was incapable of containing any more, and sent them back to the sabers of the enemy. At a greater distance, the cavalry plunged into the river, and were delivered, by being shot in the midst of it, from this scene of horror. Even such as reached the other side, or had crossed before the breaking of the bridge, were not safe. They drew themselves up in battalia to receive and protect such of their companions as should attempt the passage; but the impetuous Mandreoski, a Brigadier of horse, could not bear to see them live. He threw himself into the river, followed by his brigade; but in mid-stream he received a wound from a musket ball which deprived him of all sense. He was brought back to the place he set out from, but not until ten years after in a still more celebrated battle did he lose his life. His troops, still pursuing their point, were joined by other squadrons; and the enemy, being everywhere broken, retired for safety under the walls of Kamieniec.

The river was covered with ten thousand turbans, and the earth with twenty thousand slain, among which were eight thousand janizaries. The victory cost the Poles between five and six thousand killed and wounded. When we consider the immense superiority of the conquered army, the whole tale reads like a fable. But one of these two suppositions will account for it; either it is a great disadvantage to wait for an enemy in intrenchments, or Heaven fought on the side of the Poles. There is a third, which will perhaps give a better solution: When men fight, not for the whim of a Sovereign, but for the real interest of themselves and their country, they are raised above the common level. When they have the incentive to fight for home and country, their dearest interests and rights; when men are conscious of this, they are almost unconquerable.

The Poles took a great number of prisoners who received the treatment usually accorded to prisoners of those days, which in this day of enlightenment looks harsh and cruel. There is no better evidence of the world's progress than in the humane treatment of prisoners of war, compared with what it was in the days of Sobieski. He showed great humanity

to the wretches who waited for their fate in the citadel of Choczin, which contained vast riches, being
the place where the Greeks, Armenians and Jews
kept their magazines for the camp. The artillery
was brought up against it the same day, and it soon
capitulated.

While this was passing between the Pruth and the
Niester, the Turkish Aga proceeded on his journey;
and, arriving at Leopol about the beginning of November, found the King lying at the point of death.
An ulcer in the kidneys, blood instead of urine, con-
vulsions in his stomach, and continual vomiting, left
him so small a remnant of life, as would not permit
him to give audience. In short, Michael died on
the 10th of November, leaving no children. At the
time of the King's death he was thirty-five years of
age. He spent four years upon the throne, and
these four years were spent in uneasiness, infamy,
disturbance and horror. Probably with but a single
exception, this King was the most unfortunate of
any of the Sovereigns that were chosen to reign over
the Republic. If the crown is capable of making
any man happy, it must be him only who is able to
wield it. Michael, who was naturally of a humane
temper, would have been a good King if he had been
a great one; but he was utterly wanting in all capacity. He was entirely lacking in all the qualities
of a successful Sovereign. When he was elected

King, he cried out to those who surrounded him, " I have been elected to a position that I am incapable of filling." Whether he was sincere or not, in this declaration, he spoke the truth when he made that statement. All that he got by being exalted to the regal dignity was to be drenched with gall, without the least particle of comfort. He felt all the annoy-ance, all of the embarrassment, but none of the good; for he expired on the evening before the victory of Choczin.

The news of the King's death, being received by the army, furnished many with a fair pretense for returning home: such as were loaded with spoils of the East were impatient to lay up their booty safely; others, who were tired with the labors of so severe a season, eagerly wished for the end of it; and all alleged that the election of a new King was the only thing that should now engage the attention of the Polish nation.

Sobieski represented that the election could not come on before spring, and that the winter might be usefully employed in driving the Turks out of Uk-raine, and, perhaps, in making an attempt upon Kamieniec. It is surprising that he, who had so many claims to the crown, if merit be any claim at all, should be so little in haste to return to Warsaw and form a party in his own favor. That he wished to be king, there is no question. To be a Sovereign, a ruler of a people, a free people, an elective Sovereign, was indeed a great honor; one that no one could despise, and that Sobieski desired it, there is no question; but so devoted was he to his country and to his duty, that he could not, even in his own interests, be remiss in any one of his obligations to his country; so instead of returning to his home, he was busy in animating the Poles to new enterprises; but he was stopped by an order from the Primate, requiring him to bring the army without delay back into Poland. The will of the Interrex is more sacred than that of the King, and there was nothing left for him to do but to obey. All that the Grand-General could do was to leave a garrison at Choczin, where the Poles raised a hillock which they call Mogila, to be a rude monument of a glorious victory.

If we consider this celebrated expedition on the side of conquest, it presents no very advantageous idea. The only acquisition was Choczin, a heap of cottages covered with straw. The citadel, which was a good one for the country, was retaken by the Turks, in the winter. But if we view it on the side of glory, and as being the preservation of Poland, there are very few of equal luster, or so highly interesting. It prevented the treaty of Bouchaz from being ratified by the first payment of the tribute agreed upon; suspended the slavery of Poland; weakened the Turks by the destruction of their best army, and taught them that Poland, with only very inferior forces, was capable of braving their immense power and superior numbers.

Sobieski, covered with glory, now came to Leopol, where he received the congratulations of all the orders of the State. The most distant palatinates sent Deputies to the Deliverer of their country. Let kings be intoxicated, if they may, with the incense that is so profusely, however lacking in spontaneity, offered them after victories, in which they have commonly no share; that which Sobieski received was the tribute of deep national gratitude and joy. At the report of the triumph of Choczin every one left off mourning for a king who was not worthy of lamentation.

In the meantime Warsaw was filled with intrigues that were forming for the election of a king, but Sobieski stayed at Leopol, as if he had no pretensions. The best title to it, he must have thought, was to continue to defend his country; he, therefore, fixed his residence at Leopol for the winter, where he was in readiness to restrain the incursions of the Tartars and the Cossacks, or to endeavor, if an oppertunity offered, to win over the latter.

The Diet of Convocation which precedes that of election, was summoned to meet on the fifteenth day of January, 1674. It was to have ended in fifteen days; but the desire which every one had to see Sobieski present at it, caused it to be postponed to the 22d of February; he refused, however, to gratify this earnest wish, being wholly taken up with the enemy. Sobieski had now become, more than ever, the hero and idol of the army and of the nation. What a wonderful experience he had had! In all the world's history I think there has never been a parallel case, where a general, with the stamp of outlawry upon him, with the sentence of death imposed, has marched out at the head of an army and delivered the Republic and saved the King himself. At least I do not know of any parallel case. No wonder that the nation worshiped him. Whether he was so sanguine that he would be elected King that he need make no effort, or wholly from a patriotic desire to watch the boundaries of the Republic against the enemy, each one must determine for himself. I believe that the latter reason was why he did not appear at the Diet. Everything went on quietly in the Diet, under the direction of the Primate. The death of the King and the time of election were notified, according to custom, to the Powers of Europe; and the field of election was opened on the first of May.

Sobieski showed, or perhaps only simulated, so much indifference for the crown, that, notwithstanding the repeated instances of the Electors who had a mind to be profited by his superior talents, he did not arrive until the tenth of May. Perhaps his delay might be partially founded on policy, in order to be more taken notice of; but the entire absence in all his life of any attempt at the dramatic rather inclines the writer to believe that that was not his object. This was his first appearance before the Assembly of the Estates since the victory of Choczin; and he was received with a pomp which might well astonish the foreigners then present, who were not accustomed in their own countries to see Generals receive any such honors of triumph. In those days, however skillful the general, however great his triumphs, all the glory went to the Sovereign, but in a Republic like Poland, as in all republics, the people are more apt to show their appreciation for the one to whom they have just reasons to be indebted.

Of the six competitors for the Crown, there were four who had not even the slightest chance to ingratiate themselves in the inclinations of the voters; these were Prince Thomas of Savoy, the Duke of Modena, Prince George of Denmark and the Prince of Transylvania. The other two, Prince Charles of Lorraine and the Prince of Newberg, entered the lists.

Sobieski raised up a third party, by representing that, in the present situation of the republic, when it was on the eve of being attacked by the whole Ottoman power, it wanted a hero of tried abilities, whose bare name might be an omen of victory. That this hero would not be found in the Prince of Newburg, who had never paid his addresses to military glory, nor even in Prince Charles, who had only been honored with her first smiles, was certain. But their wants would be amply supplied by the Prince of Conde, who had received all the favors she could bestow, and was so celebrated in Europe that they ought to have given him the Crown when the throne was last vacant, without bestowing it upon a wretched libel, the authors of which dared not show themselves; but that it was not yet too late to choose themselves a king whom all the powers would be ambitious of, if they had a power to dispose of themselves.

Sobieski's proposal continued a mystery, which was not long coming to light. It was surprising that the Diet should never think of giving the Crown to him who was the Hero of Poland. But while his talents and his virtues brought him near the throne, there were two pretenses that kept him at a distance from it; Mary d'Arquien, his wife, was looked upon by the Grandees, as unworthy of that station. "That highest of all honors," said they, "is fitter for the blood of the House of Austria." Thus it is that men often sacrifice their happiness to a shadow. It seems almost incredible that the achievements of Sobieski, his great ability, and the gratitude of the nation and their unwillingness to shower their great honors in appreciation of his achievements did not cause the Diet to acknowledge him by all odds to be the candidate above all others, capable of the great trust that they would bestow; yet they stopped and hesitated simply because his wife was not popular with the Court. Another obstacle of greater weight was the positive exclusion given by the Lithuanians to every Piast: "A nation," said they, "which has suffered so much from the weak government of Michael, should look for a foreign born king." This too seems most remarkable, when it was shown that the weakest and the most incapable of her kings had been foreign Princes; and yet they forgot all of this when they remembered the last mistake they made in the election of Michael. To the Queen alone must be laid the blame for she had secretly brought about this exclusion, which was such a disgrace to Poland. The Lithuanians did not allege the true reason. The Queen and the Paz could not be persuaded that Sobieski had no design upon the Crown. He appeared in the Diet with all the magnificence of a king, and had all the merit requisite for that station; it was necessary, therefore, to exclude him, under the flimsy excuse that he bore the title of a Piast.

It was obvious that Sobieski was strong enough to make himself master of the election, being already master of the Polish army, which called loudly for

the Prince of Conde, and followed in this particular the directions of its General, without penetrat-
ing into his designs.   The Paz, with the army of
Lithuania, less numerous indeed than the other, prepared to support the interests of the Queen and
Prince Charles.   The two brothers had all the as-
cendant they could over the Lithuanians; they knew
that Prince Charles was in Silesia, with a body of
troops which, when joined to theirs, would be a
match for the Polish army.   These possibilities for
a civil war struck with horror all who sincerely loved
their country.

In this fermentation of opposite factions, Sobieski proposed a method of reconciliation, which was
fit only to embroil things still more.   Queen Eleanora should break off her engagement with Prince
Charles, and give her hand to the Prince of Newburg, from whom the Republic had more to expect,
on account of his great fortune; and upon this condition the Prince of Conde should withdraw his pretensions.   To bring this about a deputation from the
Senate waited upon the Queen, who, having engaged
her heart and her jewels to Prince Charles, showed
by her answer that she continued inviolably attached
to him; and the Ambassador of Vienna protested
loudly that his Court would never give up its Candidate.   The Grandees persisted in giving him their
votes, and he would probably have had the Crown

if Florian Czartoriski, the Primate and Interrex, had lived a few days longer. His death weakened Prince Charles' party and changed the whole phase of the election.

Andrew Trzebiski, Bishop of Cracow, a man of less warmth, took his place in the Diet of Election, and performed the function of Interrex, but could not unite the votes of the Assembly. In one part was heard the name of Prince Charles; in another the Prince of Newburg; and, louder still, that of Conde. At last the Palatine of Russia, Stanislaus Jablonowski, a Senator equally respectable for his birth and his fortune, his knowledge of the law, and his behavior in arms, who always spoke as he thought, and was a friend to Sobieski, because he loved his country, rose up and endeavored to put an end to this state of uncertainty. " If, in our choice of a king," said he, " we were to be determined by appearances only, it would be nearly equal, whether we chose the Prince of Lorraine or the Prince of Newburg; both of them have blossoms to show, but it is fruit that we want; and upon this footing I would give my suffrage to the great Conde, the Prince of France, were it not that fruit which is too ripe is on the point of decaying. Sobieski, in proposing him, considers only that blaze of glory which gilds over the *ruins* of the hero; but is his forgetting himself a reason for our following his example ? Sobieski is in person before your eyes. His age, his health, his vigor, his talents, and his fortune all speak loudly in his behalf. He was born in the same country, and educated in the same principles and sentiments with yourselves. You have often profited by his superior abilities in the Senate and the Diet, and have repeatedly been led to victory under his auspices. He has supported the Crown of Poland, and will know how to wear it. By looking out for a king among foreigners, do you mean to have it said that Poland produces no heroes of its own? By choosing out of foreign sovereign families, we have more than once brought ruin upon our country. You are discharged of all obligations towards Queen Eleanora, by her refusing the husband that was offered her; but you are still bound to your country, whose welfare depends upon your choice of Sobieski."

Scarce had Jablonowski done speaking when five palatinates — that is to say, their deputies, castellans, palatines and many other nobles — cried out, "Sobieski forever! We will all perish together or have him for our King." The Palatine of Russia, which was Sobieski's native country, distinguished itself by its zeal above the rest, and before the end of the day, the acclamation became general among the Poles; but the Lithuanians were extremely averse to this choice. There were some reasons for this, but one in particular; the scathing address of Sobieski, when they were about to desert him in battle, when they were brought to their sense of duty by his address, still seemed to rankle in their bosoms. The two Pazs quitted the Assembly abruptly, with their friends, to enter before the Register of the Chancery a protest against the election, as not being unanimous, and the reader remembers that there must be unanimity to secure election. So the crown was still in suspense during the succeeding night, which was spent in agitation and discord. Jablonowski and the Interrex did all they could to unite the suffrages. At last the two Pazs, after having spent the whole night to no purpose, in contriving methods of making the election miscarry, and reflecting upon the inferiority of their number, and the danger that might attend their obstinacy, appeared again in the field of election on the 19th of May, and Sobieski, by a unanimous consent, was proclaimed King. The *faint* and *languid* pleasure of a king who reigns by right of blood and ancestry, without any merit upon his own part, and in most cases, as the world's history shows, without any qualities of either head or heart, who reigns barely by the right of blood, is not to be compared with that of a king who is made so by the election of a free people, conferring the Crown upon the object of its love and its esteem.

Never did the Polish nation discover more joy

than upon this last occasion. The Senate, the Equestrian Order, the Army, and the people conducted the new King with civil and military pomp, with the roar of cannon and repeated acclamations to the Great Church of St. John, to return thanks to God, who had often been thanked at the same altar for kings that he had given in his anger; but the Poles now flattered themselves that they had made no mistake.

CHAPTER X

WHILE all Warsaw was filled with rejoicing, Queen Eleanora was sick out of mere convenience. The new king paid her a visit; but this king was not Prince Charles, and the throne must be resigned to Mary d'Arquien.

Eleanora's followers in the Senate attempted instantly to avenge her cause, and perhaps to give Sobieski a distaste to the throne, before he was seated in it. With this view, they drew up the Pacta Conventa, in terms which confined the expense of the King's household, and the royal authority, within narrower limits than had anciently been set to them.

Sobieski saw the designs that were laid for him and avoided them by exerting a noble spirit of disinterestedness, which always succeeds with great men. " You have chosen me," said he, " for your King, but the work is not yet completed, and I am still in a state of hesitation. The Republic has not yet delivered to me the instrument of election, nor have I yet accepted it, in that solemn form which ratifies the whole transaction; and therefore, if you show a distrust of me by laying fetters upon me, which my predecessors would have refused, I reject them and the crown together."

This generous behavior stopped the mouths of these disturbers; and the face of the Republic, after some debates, assumed at last an air of serenity and peace; and, everything being quiet, or at least seeming to be so, the new king received in form the instrument of election in the same great church to which he was conducted upon quitting the field of election.

Sobieski, at the time of his election, was forty-five years old; an age equally distant from the heat of youthful passions and the cold of old age; an age when all the talents display themselves in full luster; and, if the throne were to be given to the advantages of figure, he would have deserved it in this view also; a tall and graceful person, a full face, regular features, an aquiline nose, eyes full of fire, a frank and open countenance, made up his picture. He had not yet that bulkiness of body which in time made him less graceful; he had only that plumpness which indicates vigorous health and suits so well with the Polish habit. He derived from nature that majestic air, with which courtiers compliment every sovereign. He took the appellation of John III, a name to which the two kings, who had borne it before him, had done no honor. Mary, his Queen, was possessed of an elegant form, a majestic air, a fine complexion, sparkling eyes, a stately look, a great deal of wit; her only fault was perhaps in being a little too artful.

The Austrian queen forgave her all this, but could not forgive the loss of the throne, the luster of which could, for the future, only give her pain. A few months after she retired into Silesia, by the dircetion of the Emperor, her brother. This retreat was concealed at first under the pretense of a journey, that she might not lose her settlement; for, by the laws of Poland, whoever enjoys any advantages from the public, must be an inhabitant of the kingdom; and a very wise and just law this is. But, though she had lost the throne, there still remained Prince Charles, whom she married in 1678; and if love could have made amends to ambitious minds, Eleanora might have been fully satisfied.

The new queen, though her ambition had been so amply gratified, was yet eagerly desirous of a further object. The King was contented with having deserved the crown, but she was impatient to try it on. To hereditary kings, the coronation is a mere ceremony, which adds nothing to the authority they derive from their birth; but, to elective princes, it is a solemn and necessary act, which puts them in possession of sovereign power. The interval between the election and coronation is a continuation of the interregnum, which still leaves the government in the hands of the Primate. The new king dates his reign only from the day when he is crowned, and his hands are so tied up, that he cannot sign himself " King," without adding " elect "; just as the President of the United States of America receives no authority, no distinction, no honor, until after his inauguration.

Notwithstanding so many disadvantages, to which Sobieski might have put an end with a single word, he was more in haste to avenge his country than to reign over it. In this respect he stood not alone but in a very small company of men. He had gained the crown solely by his own merit, and he now deferred his coronation to give himself up entirely to the war against the Turks. The Republic repaid this act of generosity with another; for the law was broken through on this occasion, and he was authorized to date his reign from the day of his election; to decide peace and war. This was a generous act of the nation, but well deserved, and it also authorized him to publish universals under his privy-seal, for the assembling of the Diets and the Pospolite, in case of necessity, to send dispatches to foreign courts under the same seal; and to fill up vacant offices.

Mohammed had no design of avenging, this year, the defeat of Choczin. Cuprogli was lately dead, and some of the last words that he spoke, fixing his eyes upon the Alcoran, were these: " Prophet, I shall soon see whether thy words are true; but, be they true or false, I am sure of being happy, if virtue be the best of all religions." These memorable words can be uttered by few men, but in this case they were spoken with all sincerity. Though classed as an infidel, as the Christians called the Mohammedans, this great man had all the virtues of the men enlightened by the followers of the Nazarene. The death of this great man left the Ottoman Empire in a state of languor; and John III thought it a favorable oppertunity to reap the fruits of his victory. His first object was to recover the Ukraine; the Cossacks having given themselves to the Turks, in a mere fit of despair; and already felt the weight of their new yoke. They would not venture to make trial of the King's clemency; but, being informed that he was marching against them, and that Mohammed did not arm in their defense, they looked out for a third master, and fled by troops to the Russian territories, on the other side of the Borysthenes.

Mohammed, however, sent an order to the Cham of Tartary to defend the Ukraine with all his forces, upon pain of incurring the displeasure of the Porte.

Paz, with his Lithuanians, joined the Polish army in the beginning of September. His equal and his rival was now become his King; but the majesty of the monarch did not humble the pride of the subject. This was very characteristic of the Polish noblemen. They esteemed that one who was the maker of the

King was as great as the King himself. Paz ordered
a drum-major of his army to be hanged, for daring
to beat the general by the King's order, without waiting for his order. Hard at all times is the fate of
inferiors who come in the way of two contending
powers! John took no notice of the affront.
Whether he did right or wrong, his conduct was ap-
proved by the Senators, who were then in the army,
because they had need of Paz. The King gave up
his own resentment to the Republic; and exceeded
the promises he made at his election; for he paid the
troops with his own money during this whole campaign, and entered the Ukraine at the head of between thirty and thirty-five thousand men. Rarely,
if ever, before or since, in the world's history, has
a king or sovereign paid his army from his own
purse. Several places surrendered at the firing of
the first cannon. The monarch's clemency induced
several of the Cossacks to come over to the Polish
service; and thus a great deal of Cossack and Polish
blood was spared. Had the diplomacy of Sobieski
prevailed at the beginning of Michael's reign, all of
this valuable force would by now have been loyal to
the republic. The Cham, with a hundred thousand
Tartars, contented himself with harassing the Polish
army, but would not venture a battle.

Human, the largest and most populous town in the
Ukraine, was in daily expectation of its subsequent

fate. It contained nearly twenty thousand inhabitants, and a numerous garrison; but John III besieged and took it in the Cham's presence; and to show his contempt of the Tartar, divided his army, in order to carry on different operations at the same time; for the frost and snow gave intimation that no time was to be lost. Paz drove the Tartars before him, routed all their small parties, and favored by this means all the attempts of the army; but his zeal cooled at last and he took the road to Lithuania, contrary to the promise which he had given the King. Here, it should not be forgotten, that in Poland the authority of the King is binding only to a certain degree; the Grand-general scarce feels it at all; nevertheless, the action of the Grand-general at this critical moment of the campaign was an imperative duty.

Had it not been for this defection, the King would have completed the conquest of the Ukraine, a country which had been a scene of slaughter for thirty years together; being, therefore, no longer able to keep the field with the remnant of his forces, he distributed them among the conquered places. As for himself, instead of going to mix with his court in the pleasures of Warsaw, he fixed his winter quarters at Braclaw, a place that every one dreaded. Here he experienced the labors of royalty before he had tasted its pleasures. His presence produced two

good effects. It kept the Poles from deserting, for
they dared not murmur or even cast a look towards
Poland, when they saw the King share their fatigues.
This action is always characteristic of the great, and
later in our Civil War (the Rebellion of 1861 in the
United States of America), Grant and Sherman did
likewise. This gives heart and courage to the soldier
and inspires him with patriotism. It also restrained
the Tartars who were preparing to take advantage of
the Pazs' defection, and the extreme rigor of the
season. No horses in the world are comparable to
those of the Tartars for bearing fatigue, and the Tartars are at least as hardy as their horses.

The Cham, seeing the Polish army diminished and
separated, gave his son, Sultan Galga, a part of his
forces, in order to attack the Poles on the side of
Human and Raskow, while he himself fell upon
Braclaw and Kalnik. He even undertook the siege
of the latter place, and employed the Cossacks on
that service; for the Tartars never make war but on
horseback. But Sobieski did not give him time to
carry on his work; he presented himself in the fight
of the Tartars, and the siege was raised.

At last, the Cham resolved to close all with a decisive blow. Sultan Galga had met with such a reception everywhere, that he dared not make any
attempt; the Cham, therefore, united all his forces,
and appeared before the gates of Braclaw, where

Sobieski had shut himself up with a small force. The Cham's design was either to draw him from behind the walls, or to leave him the mortification of not daring to come out. But the King suffered him to dance attendance for some days; and, at a time when he least expected it, made a sally with his cavalry; attacked him, saber in hand, and the Cham lost two thousand men and many prisoners in an hour's time.

The Cham, being worsted upon all occasions, and unable to obtain booty in a country which he was ordered to defend, retired to his own dominions, and left the Poles in peace; but this peace was soon to be succeeded by a greater alarm than ever.

CHAPTER XI

MOHAMMED, at length, reused himself from his inertness, and devoted his thoughts to revenge. The breaking of the treaty of Bouchaz, the defeat at Choczin, the insolence of the Poles, whom he considered nothing more nor less than a conquered people; their real weakness, and the greatness of his own strength; all served to provoke him. The general, to whom he had entrusted his revenge, was Kara-Mustapha, a mere courtier, educated in the seraglio, who, by the charms of his person, had gained the good graces of the Sultana Valike. The rendezvous was appointed at Bender, the place where Charles XII, though a prisoner, still made himself feared.

The triumphs of the King hindered the distresses of the Republic from being felt; but they were now aggravated beyond measure and every one murmured against him as the author of the war. Discourses of this sort, under an absolute monarchy, pass off like a fleeting cloud. The monarch, whether he hears them or not, ruins or saves his own people in his own way. But, in a mixed government, the King must

subdue his own subjects by reason, before he can conquer his enemies by force.

In order to allay the apprehensions of Poland, the
King quitted the Ukraine, after leaving garrisons behind him, and led the rest of his troops to Leopol,
about the close of April, 1675. His army, if it
deserved that name, was much diminished by sieges,
skirmishes, the severity of the winter, and disorders.
He raised recruits in the greatest haste, but was
forced to drag them out of the arms of consternation
and discontent. IIis power over the minds of men
must have been most extraordinary and equal to his
reputation, or the Republic would never have con-
sented to expose itself with him. He sent orders to
the Lithuanians to join him immediately, after having written to the Grand-general Paz in a style that
was likely to make an impression on him; and then
formed his plan of action. Judging of the Vizier's
abilities by his own, and a wise man always does that,
he doubted not of seeing him fall upon the palatinate
of Russia, which would open a way into the heart of
Poland. Upon this supposition, be entrusted the
wise Jablonowski with six thousand men, and ordered him to intrench himself under the cannon of
Zloczew, that he might guard that pass. He had
only twelve thousand men left to sustain the weight
of the war. Leopol, though a weak and wretched
fortress, was yet of the utmost importance, as it cov-

ered Russia and the neighboring provinces. At the
gates of this city, King John sat down to wait for
the enemy, and was greatly astonished when he
heard, in the beginning of July, that the Vizier had
entered the Ukraine to throw away his time in be-
sieging Human, instead of advancing instantly to
crush the little army of the King, that on this occasion was so small and insignificant that it would
seem that the first object he could have had would
have been the destruction of this army with its great
leader, and then he could do what he desired at
pleasure, for it would have left Poland at his mercy.
The quick eye of Sobieski detected this great mistake
of his opponent, and no one could have seen the mistake of an enemy quicker than Sobieski, and he exclaimed, " Since he knows no better than this, I will
give a good account of his army, before the end of
the campaign."

The defense of the city was at that time a great
responsibility. In a war among the Powers of Europe, the worst that happens when a city is surrendered is to continue a prisoner of war till an
exchange be settled; but, between the Turks and the
Poles, the mildest fate is perpetual slavery, which
to a brave man is more terrible than death itself;
from Kara-Mustapha there was reason to dread the
worst of horrors.

Human held out fifteen days against this great

army. The artillery of the Turks was of an enormous weight, and their threats terrible. At length, the place, having several breaches in its walls, and being without hope of succor, was compelled to surrender; but the Vizier, with a barbarity scarce to be pardoned when a town is taken by storm, glutted himself with blood. Twenty thousand souls perished in this awful slaughter; and many an infant was seen vomiting up milk, mixed with blood, upon its mother's breast. The Vizier's design was unquestionably to frighten Poland, and subdue it by means of terror.

Human had cost him too great an expense of time and men to undertake more sieges in the Ukraine; he therefore turned towards the left, and advanced by quick marches into Podolia. The same acts of cruelty were repeated everywhere and it produced two different effects: The pusillanimous surrendered at the first attack, in order to save their lives; but the courageous sought only to die with arms in their hands.

This last was the character of him who defended Sharas, a large castle covered with outworks, situated upon a hill, and making part of the large domain of Wicsnowieski, petty-general of the Polish army, who had garrisoned it with six hundred foot, commanded by Des Auteuils, a French nobleman. It was not easy to put the place into better hands.

He defended himself with vigor for two weeks, while the Vizier raved and threatened at his usual rate. There were several noble families who had taken refuge in the castle and pressed Des Auteuils to surrender; but he was deaf to the suggestions of fear and threatened to turn them out of the place if he heard any more of this cowardly proposal. The wretches said no more; but, taking an opportunity when Des Auteuils could make no resistance, they gave him several mortal wounds, and threw him over the walls. The Vizier himself was struck with horror at this act of villainy; and covering his natural cruelty with the mask of justice, he cut off every head that he found in the place, to revenge the death of the commander. I am of the opinion that the Vizier, in this instance, was actuated purely from the best of impulses. A traitor is always despised, a coward is hated of God and man, and when this was coupled with the assassination of the brave defender, it was too terrible and contemptible even for the Turk, and in this way he showed his opinion of them.

The barbarian by these bloody conquests was only preparing a way for a complete victory that he had planned in his own mind. When he sat down before Sbaras, he detached fifty thousand men, under the command of Sultan Nuradin, with orders to attack the King without giving quarter to any one, and to spread destruction on all sides as he marched.

The King's army, which was encamped at Leopol, had received some additions. The whole amounted to fifteen thousand men. Paz, though the danger was extreme, made no haste to join the King with his Lithuanians. It must be ever borne in mind that the Lithuanians are really not Poles. They became a part of Poland by the marriage of their Prince with the celebrated Polish Queen, Hedwig, and this will account, to a great extent, for the seeming indifference of their commander in many campaigns, and was often an occasion of embarrassment to the King.

It is astonishing that the Vizier, instead of employing himself in taking weak places, did not come in person to give battle to the King. This was the affair of honor, the capital point which would determine all the rest. The Tartar whom he charged with this commission had no contemptible reputation, and in a way he was considered one of their ablest soldiers; the best thing, however, that he did, and this is important indeed in the commander, was to advance with great rapidity. His march resembled a devouring fire; all the villages and hamlets were burned by his order. He appeared as quick as lightning before Jablonowski's little camp. He even made an attempt upon the intrenchments; but that general soon convinced him that it would not be an easy matter to gain any advantage over him, and the

Tartar had a mind to preserve all his forces for a more important campaign. The quickness of his march, and his care to intercept all the Polish couriers were so well conducted that, had it not been for the flames which drew near to Leopol, the King, who was never before surprised, would have been now. Early in the morning, the Poles perceived the enemy's army, consisting wholly of Turkish and Tartarian horse, in a vast plain ending at the foot of the mountains. Though it was only the month of August, it snowed hard; there fell also a heavy shower of hail, which happened to incommode the Infidels more than the Christians. All the priests, bishops, and bad philosophers in the Christian army cried out, " A miracle," and the memoirs of that time credulously state that it really was one. The King made use of it to inspire his little army with confidence, without neglecting the precautions of human prudence. He did not wait for the enemy in his camp, but ascended the rising grounds where he ordered the Towarisz to plant their lances upon the highest summit, in order to appear more numerous to the enemy, who had already reached the foot of the mountains. He ordered his own regiment of dragoons to descend the hill, in small parties, under cover of the bushes; and these dragoons, by firing at a very small distance, forced the enemy's vanguard to retire. A Polish squadron filled the first vacaney; others pressing on, formed in the same manner; and the whole army was soon drawn up in battle array, while the lances of the Towarisz were still to be seen upon the eminences.

The Infidels, seeing no more troops coming down and trusting to their superior number, began the charge with cries and howlings which probably would have had fatal effects upon an army that heard them for the first time, but the Poles felt no terror at the noise of their enemies; although their attack was really dreadful and made them stagger. The King restored order and suffered the Infidels to throw away their first fire. They returned to the attack several times and the Poles contented themselves with giving them a warm reception. The King had placed a body in ambuscade to take them in flank, and a battery was advancing upon a hill to play upon them. This was the moment for which the King had waited to attack them in his turn. Never was there a general more determined, nor did the Polish troops ever display greater valor. The Infidels, being attacked in front and in flank, gave way at the second charge and from this instant the confusion increased among them. They were pursued to a deep morass where a great number perished. They left between fourteen and fifteen thousand upon the field of battle, and night saved the rest. Nuradin had boasted that he would take the

King prisoner and present him to the Vizir, but he narrowly escaped being taken himself and carried the news of his own defeat to the camp at Sharas.

The Vizier, struck with consternation, resolved upon finishing the campaign with some important blow; it was not by marching in person against the conqueror and wresting from him his victory, but by taking Trembowla, at the entrance of Podolia, a fortress with large and strong outworks, hanging upon a rock, the access to which is practicable only in one place which leads to a little plain covered with a thick wood. In order to succeed the sooner in his design and spare the blood of the janizaries, he made use of art before he had recourse to violence. He was uneasy at the reputation of the Governor, Samuel Chrasonowski, a renegade Jew who had quitted the laws of Moses for that of Jesus and was more zealous against his brethren of the circumcision than if he had never undergone that operation himself. The Vizir employed a Polish prisoner, Makowiski, to represent to him by letters " that it would be rash to persist obstinately in the defense of a place that must eventually be taken and that he ought rather think of deserving the victor's clemency than provoking his wrath."

Chrasonowski returned a double answer; one to Makowiski, in these terms: " I am not at all surprised that, being in irons, thou hast the soul of a slave; but what astonishes me is the daring to talk of the Vizier's clemency, after what has happened to several places and thyself. Farewell: All the harm I wish thee is that thou mayest live long in the infamy and servitude thou deservest. Annihilation would be to thee a blessing but thou hast not the courage to confer it upon thyself."

The answer to the Vizier was not less haughty: "Thou art mistaken if thou expectest to find gold within these walls; we have nothing here but steel and soldiers; our number indeed is small but our courage is great. Do not flatter thyself that we will surrender for thou shalt never take us till we have all breathed our last. I am preparing to give thee another answer by the mouth of my cannon."

The Vizier, white with rage, ordered the place to be assaulted with all imaginable fury. The place defended itself beyond what could be expected, and the wife of the Jewish Governor, equally beautiful with Judith and more enterprising, having no opportunity, like her, to cut off the head of the Vizir while he slept, made great havoc of the Turks in sallies conducted by herself; filled up their trenches and fought upon the breach. But what can the brave do, when the cowards are more numerous and demand surrender?

Chrasonowski had the same inconvenience to struggle with, which had been the destruction of

Des Auteuils and Sharas.   The nobility who had taken refuge in the place, seeing a breach made and grow wider every hour, and dreading the implacable fury of the Vizir if they stood a storm, lost courage. Their despair was the greater as they expected no relief; but they were mistaken in this particular, for the Lithuanian army had at length joined the Poles in the camp before Leopol.   The King was upon his march and, by calling in, upon the way, the small body under Jablonowski, his strength amounted to thirty-three thousand men, but, as there was no news at Trembowla of this relief, it had no effect in the present critical juncture.   Instead of continuing to defend themselves, as they had hitherto done, the nobles communicated their apprehensions and fears to the officers of the garrison.   The Jewish heroine heard their consultations from a place where she could not be perceived and there she learned that they were fully determined to surrender.   She at once flew to her husband and acquainted him with it, in the thickest of the fire.   The brave commander ran to this assembly of cowards: *"It is by no means certain,"* said he, *"that the enemy will over-power us; but it is absolutely true that I will blow you up in this very room if you persist in your base design.   There are soldiers at the door, with their matches lighted, on purpose to execute my orders."* The prospect of inevitable death put arms again into their hands and they endeavored to wipe off this stain.

The Vizier was not ignorant that the King was marching to relieve the town and therefore hastened his attack. The place had already been assaulted four times and Chrasonowski, himself, feared what the fifth might do. His wife mistook this just concern for a mark of weakness that boded no good. A woman, once over the natural timidity of her sex, becomes more than man. This Roman of the North, armed with two poniards, said to her husband: " One of these is destined for thee, if thou surrenderest the town; the other I intend for myself."

It was in this moment of distress that the Polish army arrived. The Vizier raised the siege, not daring to try his fortune against that of the King, but he was forced to it in this event, because he took his measures too late. He repassed the Janow, a river near the town, with all haste; but half his army being still on this side of the river, King John attacked it finally, crying out to the foremost squadrons, " that he required nothing of them but that he would set them an example of himself." Indeed this had distinguished him in all his battles and in all his campaigns; to make himself one with his army, shirking nothing, never hesitating, particularly in danger and exposure. The battle lasted a long while and the Turks lost eight thousand men and retired, in dismay and consternation, under the cannon of Kamieniec.

The garrisons of the places which the Turks had captured did not wait for the vengeance of the Poles, but abandoned them to go and rejoin the army. Trembowla owed its deliverance to the intrepidity of Chrasonowski and gratefully confessed it. He himself was raised to military honors; his wife contented herself with the applauses of the nation. No woman ever deserved it more than this brave, more than Spartan, woman and, for the time being, all of the absurd prejudices against her race and her religion were forgotten. They only thought of her magnificent womanhood and proclaimed her as a heroine of the nation.

Kara-Mustapha was now taught that superior numbers, cruelty, and presumption are not sufficient to insure victory. He staid some time at Kamieniec and then directed his march towards the Danube. This campaign had served to teach nations of inferier strength not to despair when they have a great leader at their head.

The army now retired into winter quarters and King John went to repose himself at Zolkiew, a town in the palatinate of Russia, nine miles from Leopol, which made part of the estate of the Zolkiewskis, his ancestors on the mother's side.

CHAPTER XII

IN the meantime, Warsaw was impatient to enjoy again the presence of its King. The eighteen months which had passed since his election he had employed in a manner that made him still more worthy of the crown; but the crown was not yet resting upon his noble head. He therefore complied with the wishes of his capital and his coronation was fixed for the second of May, 1676.

Persons who are fond of magnificent displays, and do not consider what they cost the public, would have been struck with the splendor of this. All the magnificence of Asia was seen united with all the elegance of Europe. Slaves from Ethiopia and the East, clothed in azure habits; young Poles in purple robes, a whole army dressed to the greatest advantage; the equipages, men and horses contending with each other in splendor; the gold eclipsed by jewels. Such was the procession in the midst of which Sobieski appeared upon a Persian horse, going to take possession of a crown which he had earned by his virtues.

Mohammed, full of wrath and indignation at a little Republic that dared to contend with him, ordered an army of a hundred and twenty thousand Turks and eighty thousand Tartars, making a total of two hundred thousand, to avenge the honor of the crescent. The command of this army was given to Ibrahim Shaitan, a man of cool valor, great experience, and a second Ulysses for stratagem. The surname of Shaitan, which signifies "Devil," was intended to express this last quality. Notwithstanding the victories of her King, Poland was still upon the brink of ruin. Thirty-eight thousand fighting men were assembled near Leopol, and, with this small number, King John marched against two hundred thousand. After a variety of fortune on both sides, yet without coming to any decisive battle, the King found means to have an honorable peace ratified for Poland, which was signed on the 29th day of October of the same year.

Ibrahim had not yet done all that he could with so great a force; but King John had done much more than could possibly be expected. When he passed the Niester, to stop two such armies upon the frontiers, all Europe accused him of rashness and gave him over for lost. But heroes judge better of one another; the great Conde admired his conduct and congratulated him on it by letter.

And yet, when we reflect on the cause of so long a war, who is there that will dare to be an advocate for severity? The Cossacks complained of oppression, were not listened to, and revolted. Common justice and mild treatment would have quieted the commotion. Wild and war-like and impatient of restraint as the Cossacks were, they yielded readily to kindness and to justice, but, alas! Poland was no exception to the tendency of a nation toward a conquered people. Such conduct has invariably been one of oppression; rigor involved their governors in a war of thirty-eight years' continuance. The Turks took part in the quarrel and every campaign seemed to open the grave of Poland. At length the catastrophe came, and gave occasion for deploring equally the power of princes and the misery of subjects. In four campaigns, Mohammed lost more than two hundred thousand men, and expended sums sufficient to have relieved millions of unhappy persons. By so great a waste of men and money, what advantages did he reap? A few places in Podolia and the Ukraine, which he was not sure of possessing for any length of time.

On the other side, Poland thought itself sufficiently recompensed for all the ravages, burnings, depopulations and horrors it had suffered by being delivered from the tribute yielded by a weak, impotent king and nobles; at the time Sobieski was not in council, but was fighting the battles of Poland, turning back another great army that threatened to overwhelm his country, and all this sentence of death still upon him. No wonder Poland, with Sobieski for king, felt amply repaid!

CHAPTER XIII

IT was now a long time that the Republic had supported itself by dint of arms. At length it began to take breath under the laurels with which its hero had crowned it and the seven succeeding years were years of peace. During this period, some domestic affairs and negotiations with foreign Powers deserve our notice; but, as they come short of the glory our ideas generally annex to military exploits we shall still consider the King in that capacity.

In 1680 King John turned towards the House of Austria, from which he expected great assistance in an expedition the plan of which he had laid. He knew, by his intelligence in the seraglio, that Mohammed intended to attack the Emperor Leopold, but as yet it was only a project, as the Turks generally make immense armaments, there is time for action while they are getting ready. He knew also that Mohammed, depending upon the late treaty with Poland, had left Kamieniec and Podolia without any great defense.

The loss of the former was incessantly regretted by the Republic, and its recovery would bring great glory to the King, for let the reader remember that this stronghold of the Republic had been in the possession of the Turks and it was an eyesore to the King. Mohammed indeed had reason to be without apprehension, if treaties between Christians and Infidels are obligatory; but people form their ideas of morality upon the principles of the age, and the place in which they live. Rome was always ready to absolve the Poles from the oaths they had sworn to the Turks. Indeed this has ever been the shame and disgrace of our so-called Christian civilization, whether treating with nations of unbelievers or whether treating with conquered tribes, while we extract from them to the uttermost, we never hesitate at any time when it suits our convenience to break treaties, break oaths, and disregard our word of honor. The King saw, therefore, that if he could prevail upon Leopold, who was threatened by Mohammed, to be beforehand with him, he should have time to seize Kamieniec on a sudden, under a promise of uniting afterwards his arms to those of Leopold. He thought further of engaging in the league, the Republic of Venice for a diversion by sea, and Rome for a supply of money.

At all events Leopold and John resolved to unite their arms by a treaty both defensive and offensive. The Emperor engaged to furnish an army of sixty thousand men to act in Hungary, and the King of Poland, forty thousand, to be employed where it should be thought proper. The two Sovereigns were to march to each other's assistance as occasion required and whoever of the two should happen to be with the army was to be Commander in Chief. This last article gave it in effect to King John, for Leopold was no warrior.

In the beginning of May, 1683, intelligence was received that the Ottoman forces were arriving out of Asià and Africa, in the vast and fertile plains of Adrianople, their usual place of rendezvous when they marched against the Christians. Mohammed came thither with his Court, in order to be nearer the scene of war and to give more life to the expedition. He might have attacked the empire of Germany, before the peace of Nimeguen, when Leopold was engaged with Lonis XIV, and then the empire must have been destroyed. The Porte has been generally unfortunate in choosing its time to attack the Christians, who, by tearing one another to pieces so frequently, seem to present themselves to its strokes. But, after all, if the danger was less now than before the peace of Nimeguen, it was still sufficiently great.

The General of the Ottoman forces was the Grand-Vizir Kara-Mustapha, the same who had already tried his fortunes against Sobieski at Trembowla and Leopol. He still continued in favor with the Sultana Valide; and, having also gained the high regard of Mohammed, had lately married his daughter.

The Sultan does not give to every Vizier his Catis-
cherif, that is to say, a full power; but the present
had that honor conferred upon him, and perhaps never
more unworthily so; a general who had hardly ever
won a battle, who had done nothing to merit any such
honor, he had received this distinguished token of
regard from Mohammed from pure favoritism.
Never had ambition and pride, two passions that de-
voured him, a more extensive field in which to act. A
hundred and forty thousand regular troops consisting
of janizaries, Spahis and others; eighteen thousand
Wallachians, Moldavians and Transylvanians, commanded by their respective Princes; fifteen thousand Hungarians, led by Tekeli; fifty thousand Tartars, commanded by Selim-Gerai, their Cham; and,
if we include volunteers, officers of the baggage and
provisions, workmen of all sorts and personal servants, the whole must have amounted to more than
three hundred thousand men, thirty-one Bashaws,
five Sovereign Princes, with three hundred pieces of
cannon; and the object of this mighty armament was
equally great, the conquest of the western Empire.

The Imperial troops were commanded by Charles
V, Duke of Lorraine, the same who was Sobieski's
competitor for the crown of Poland in 1674. He
was then young, but had already given proofs of
having the soul of a hero. The Duke's capacity,
much more than his rank, procured him the command

in chief which would have frightened any man but himself, for he had only thirty-seven thousand men to oppose that torrent of Infidels which came to overwhelm the Empire.

The Vizir advanced on the right side of the Danube, passed the Save and the Drave, forced the Duke before him and made a feint of attacking Raab while he detached fifty thousand Tartars on the road towards Vienna. The Duke, perceiving the stratagem, made a stolen march in his turn; suffered a check at Patronel, and had scarce time to reach Vienna, where he threw in part of his infantry to reënforce the garrison and took post in the island of Leopoldstadt, formed by the Danube on the north side of the city; while the Tartars arrived about the same time on the south.

Upon this occasion was seen one of those spectacles which ought to be a lesson to Sovereigns and which move the compassion of their subjects, even when the Sovereigns have ill deserved their tenderness; Leopold, the most powerful Emperor since Charles V, flying from his capital with the Empress, his mother-in-law, the Empress, his wife, the Archduke, the Archduchesses, and a great part of the inhabitants following the Court in great disorder.

The whole country was filled with flying parties, equipages and wagons laden with goods — the last of which fell into the hands of the Tartars, at the very gates of Lintz. Even this city, which the Imperial family fled to in their first flight, did not seem a safe asylum, and they were forced to take refuge in Passaw. They lay the first night in a wood where the Empress, who was far advanced in her pregnancy, found that it was possible to sleep upon straw, surrounded on all sides by terror. Among the other horrors of this night, they had a view of the flames which already consumed Lower Hungary, and advanced towards Austria. The Turks were to be dreaded only as civilized warriors, who conquer by dint of valor; but the Tartars burned, murdered, and carried into slavery. They knew nothing of tenderness, of love, of mercy or of compassion. The deepest caves afforded an insecure retreat; the trembling victims were discovered by dogs trained to hunt men; and Tekeli, the Chief of the Hungarians, upon this occasion, was a very Tartar.

The Emperor, by only the first excesses that attended this eruption, paid dearly for his acts of violence in Hungary, and the blood of its Nobles that he had spilt. He could not be persuaded that Kara-Mustapha would leave behind him such places as Raab and Comora and fall directly upon Vienna. The King of Poland, who knew better, as is always the case with those who make war in person, gave him warning of it but without effect.

Vienna had become, under ten successive Emperors

of the House of Austria, the capital of the Roman
Empire in the West.   Solyman, the Great, was the
first Turkish Emperor that marched against Vienna
in 1529, after having been crowned King of Persia
at Bagdad, making Europe and Asia tremble at the
same time.   He failed in his attempt not daring to
contend against the fortune of Charles V, who
marched to its relief with an army of eighty thousand men.   Kara-Mustapha, who saw only a handful to oppose him, flattered himself that he should be
more fortunate and began the siege on the seventh
of July.   The Germans are undoubtedly a brave
people, but they have never appeared before the gates
of Constantinople as the Turks have before those
of Vienna.

The Vizir pitched his camp in the plain on the
southern side of the Danube and filled its whole
extent, which is nine miles.   This camp abounded
with everything that was necessary for so vast a multitude, money, ammunition and provisions of every
kind.   The different quarters were commanded by
Bashaws, who displayed the magnificence of Kings;
but all this magnificence was eclipsed by the pomp of
the Vizir, who simply wallowed in luxury.   A Grand
Vizir's retinue usually consists of two thousand officers and servants, but the present had double that
number.   His park, that is to say, the space inclosed
by his tents, near the palace of the Favorite, was

as extensive as the city he besieged. The luster of the richest stuffs of gold and jewels seemed to contend with the highly polished glare of arms. It was furnished with baths, gardens, fountains and even curious animals for his amusement. He shut himself up with his young Icoglans oftener than with his General Officers. The Iman, or Minister of religion, who attended him in this expedition, threatened him with the divine indignation, but the Vizir laughed at his menaces, and plunged himself deeper in debauchery.

In the meantime the luxury of the General did not in the least diminish the valor of the janizaries, nor was the Turkish artillery at all less formidable.

Count Staremberg, a man of abilities and experience, who was now Governor of Vienna, and had formerly been so to his Master, had set fire to the suburbs, and by a cruel necessity, burned the substance of the citizens, whom his object was to preserve. He had a garrison under him which was computed at sixteen thousand men, but in fact amounted only to eleven thousand at most.

The Duke of Lorraine, who had taken post on the island of Leopoldstadt and did his utmost to preserve a communication from thence with the city, thought himself obliged to retire from it, by the bridges which he had laid across the Danube and now ordered to be broken down. Never was there a general in a more desperate situation. For, after he had thrown part of his infantry into Vienna, Raab and Comora, he had not thirty thousand men left to keep the field.

The Turks did not get possession of the counter-scrap till the seventh of August, after repeated engagements for twenty-three days together, with great loss of blood on both sides. Their mines, their continual attacks, the decrease of the garrison, the waste of provisions, all contributed to give the utmost uneasiness; and to so many real evils more imaginary ones were added.

The Duke of Lorraine wrote letter after letter to the King of Poland to hasten his march. Notwithstanding all the diligence he had used, his army could not be got together till towards the end of the month of August, 1683. He sent away the first bodies that arrived, and while the main body was getting ready, took up his residence at Cracow, where he did not throw away his time. His fondness for hunting, play and entertainments, never showed itself, but when the Republic was at peace. He examined into the details that he received of the siege; studied the situation of Vienna by a topographical map; considered the position of the Turks in every view; settled his order of battle and regulated his marches in order to fix the decisive day.

When he arrived at Tarnowitz, the first town of Siberia, he reviewed his army which amounted only to twenty-five thousand men and, consequently, far short of the number stipulated in the treaty. Before the review was over, he received a letter from the Emperor. A copy of it may serve to show the power of adversity upon haughty minds, and the return of their pride as soon as the danger was past. "We are convinced (says the Emperor), that, by reason of the vast distance of your army, it is absolutely impossible for it to come in time enough to contribute to the preservation of the place which is in the most imminent danger. It is not therefore your troops, Sire, that we expect, but your Majesty's own presence; being fully persuaded that if your Royal person will vouchsafe to appear at the head of our forces, though less numerous than those of the enemy, your name alone, which is so justly dreaded by them, will make their defeat certain."

It must certainly have cost Leopold a great deal to make this condescension. As soon as he despaired of seeing the Polish army, nothing hindered him from putting himself at the head of his own troops; but the past and the present made him feel the necessity of another commander to whom he no longer scrupled to attribute the qualities of a hero, or to accede the title of *Majesty,* which he had before refused him. The Emperor concluded his letter with a minute account of all the troops that he was assembling, and which were to arrive forthwith at the bridge where they were to pass the Danube, assuring the King that the bridge was already finished. The sequel will show that the Emperor soon altered his language in regard to King John, and was mistaken in his facts. His letter is preserved to this day in the archives of Poland.

CHAPTER XIV

THE critical situation of affairs, and the confidence which Leopold reposed in the Polish ruler determined the King to take a step which exposed his own person to danger.

Leaving his army to the care of the Grand-general Jablonowski, he resolved to go forward himself, according to Leopold's request, and even to give battle without it if the preservation of Vienna required it. In order to get thither, he had no route to take but across Silesia, Moravia, and that part of Austria which lies to the north of the Danube; three provinces that were infested by Hungarians, Turks and Tartars whom the Duke of Lorraine, with all his splendid ability and courage, despaired of keeping within bounds any longer. The King, in his march, had only two thousand cavalrymen. Other kings, even in the midst of an army, have a second army for their guard. His equipage was no greater than that of the brave soldiers that marched with him. Here was another instance of the democratic spirit of the great King which endeared him so much to his soldiers; he did not claim for himself more than he would concede to them. Nothing but a chaise attended him, which even Prince James, his own son, made no use of; they both traveled all the way on horseback. It is not every king that is formed to be a hero; indeed very few of them, but whoever is animated with that glorious ambition must be able to endure fatiguing marches, suffer hardships and expose himself to dangers like a common soldier, whenever occasion requires it. Napoleon the Great, of more modern days, was a fair example of this. John III was so far from discovering any fear that he himself recovered the whole country from its consternation. The peasants, who had sown only that they might not reap, and regretted the fate of their massacred friends, ran together from every hamlet to see their Deliverer, and considered themselves as already delivered. His own troops that he had conducted through so many dangers, stood also in need of being encouraged, and he saw to it that no opportunity was left unimproved to strengthen and encourage them. One morning, when he was a few miles from Olmutz, an eagle flew by him on the right, and, as the Poles had retained some faith in omens, he told them a story out of the Roman history, and the flight of an eagle was considered as a token of victory. Another day, upon the weather's clearing up, after a thick mist, an inverted rainbow (a phenomenon not common, but which sometimes happens) was seen upon the surface of a meadow. The reader will bear in mind that the symbol of the Turkish power was the crescent, and this rainbow formed a crescent, but was upside down. The soldiers fancied it to be miraculous, and the King did all he could to confirm them in this belief.

At length, the King reached the banks of the Danube which it was impossible to pass by the bridges of Vienna, in sight of the enemy. He therefore marched to Tulu, a small town on the right side of the river, fifteen miles from Vienna. Leopold had written to John that the bridge at Tuln was finished, whereas, they were now at work upon it. The same letter told him that he would find the German troops assembled in readiness; but he saw only the Duke of Lorraine's little army and two battalions that guarded the head of the bridge. At this sight he broke out in a passion: " Does the Emperor take me for an adventurer? I have left my own army because he assured me that his was ready. Is it for myself, or him, that I come to fight? " The Duke, whose prudence was equal to his valor, quieted his indignation.

The Polish army was left at a great distance; and yet, to the amazement of every one, it arrived before the Germans. The quickness of its march did great honor to the Grand-general Jablonowski who made his appearance on the fifth of September.

The German Generals, leaving their troops behind, were come to attend the King and could not help expressing some disquiet at the great day that was approaching: "Consider," says the King, contemptuously, "the General you have to deal with, and not the multitude that he commands. Which of you at the head of two hundred thousand men would have suffered this bridge to be built within fifteen miles of his camp? This man has no ability to command. We shall conquer him easily."

The Polish army was, by this time, passing the bridge. The cavalrymen were universally admired for their horses, their dress and fine appearance. This was probably one of the most remarkable bodies of cavalry that ever appeared upon a field of battle. Every man was a nobleman, that is, each possessed a title of nobility; every one of them was a knight and commanded by their King, the most knightly man of that age or any other age. The infantry, however, was not so well clothed, and did not make so good an appearance. One battalion among the rest being remarkably ill-clad, Prince Lubormirski advised the King, for the honor of the nation, to let it pass in the night. The King was of a different opinion, and when the battalion was crossing the bridge he exclaimed: "Look at it well; it is an invincible body that has taken an oath never to wear any clothes but what it takes from the enemy. In the last war they were clad in the Turkish costumes." If this encomium did not furnish them with clothes, it certainly armed them with courage.

The Poles, when they had crossed the bridge, extended themselves upon the right and were exposed for twenty-four hours together to be cut in pieces, if Kara-Mustapha had known how to make the most of his advantages. At length the bodies of German troops arrived, one after another, and the whole Christian army was assembled by the 7th to the amount of seventy-four thousand men.

From the camp at Tuln, they heard the roar of the Turkish batteries. Vienna was reduced to the last extremity, and many officers of the first merit had lost their lives. The grave continued open, without ever closing its mouth. The dysentery, a disorder as destructive as the sword, carried off sixty persons a day. Staremberg himself was attacked by it. There were not more than three or four officers left to a battalion; most of these were wounded; and nearly all of their chief officers were gone. The soldiers, worn out with fatigue and bad rations, could scarcely walk to the bridge; and those who escaped the fire of the enemy died of weakness. The citizens, who at first partook in all the labors of the siege, had recourse to prayer as their only defense, and ran in crowds to the churches where the bombs and balls carried terror with them.

The Duke of Lorraine had just received a letter from Staremberg who, in the beginning of the siege,

had the firmness and even confidence to write, " I
will not surrender the place, but with the last drop
of my blood." What a splendid contrast was the
spirit of this noble commander compared with that
of the cowardly, craven Emperor Leopold! At
present he had scarce a gleam of hope remaining.
His letter contained only these words: " No more
time to lose, my Lord, no more time to lose."

The stupid inaction of Kara-Mustapha cannot be
accounted for, except that it was a spirit of over-con-
fidence. It is certain that if at this time he had
made a general attack, Vienna must have fallen.
But avarice extinguished the thunder that he held
in his hand. He entertained a notion that the place
of residence of the Emperors of Germany must con-
tain immense treasures; and he was afraid that he
should lose this imaginary wealth by the city's being pillaged, as it inevitably would be, if taken by
storm. He chose therefore to stay till the place surrendered; an event which, he continued to flatter
himself, would occur at any hour. Nor did his presumption contribute less to blind him than his avarice. He jested at the weakness of the Christian
army, which he thought still weaker than it was, and
could not suppose it would have the boldness to come
and attack him. His intelligence was so bad that he
was still ignorant of King John's coming in person.
Of all the Princes in the league, the Vizier dreaded

him the most, and we shall soon see that he had just cause.

The King, when he was just going to march, gave out the order of battle with his own hand; the following is a copy of it, as found among his manuscripts:

" The center is to consist of the Imperial troops to which we shall add the regiment of cavalry belonging to the Chevalier Lubormirski, Marshal of the Court, and four or five squadrons of our horse-guards; in the room of which we expect to have dragoons, or other German troops. This body is to be commanded by the Duke of Lorraine.

" The Polish army, commanded by the Grand-general, Jablonowski, and the other Generals of that nation, is to make the right wing.

" The troops belonging to the Electors of Bavaria and Saxony are to be placed on the left wing, to which we shall add also some squadrons of our horse guards, and other Polish cavalry, instead of which they are to give us dragoons on foot.

" The cannon is to be divided, and, in case the Electors have not enough, the Duke of Lorraine is to furnish them with some of his. This wing is to consist entirely of the troops belonging to the Electors.

" The troops of the circles of the Empire are to extend along the Danube with the left wing, inclin-

ing a little towards the right; and this, for two reasons: First, to keep the enemy in alarm, for fear
of being charged in flank; and, secondly, to be in
readiness to throw the enemy into the city, in case
we should not make an impression upon the enemy
so soon as we hope. This body is to be commanded
by the Prince of Waldec.

" The first line is to consist wholly of foot, with artillery, and to be followed closely by a line of horse.
If these two lines were to be mixed, they would embarrass each other in passing the defiles, woods and
mountains; but, as soon as we enter the plain, the
cavalry is to take post in the intervals between the
battalions, which shall be left for that purpose. This
order is to be observed particularly by our own horse
guards, which shall charge first.

" If we draw up all our troops in three lines only,
we shall take up more than a German league and a
half, which would not be for our advantage; and,
besides, we must, in this case, pass the little river of
Vien, which ought to be left on our right. We must
therefore make four lines; and the fourth will serve
for a body of reserve.

" For the greater security of the infantry against
the first attack of the Turkish horse, which is always
very warm, great use might be made of spancherais-
tres or chevaux-de-frize; but they must be very light
in order to be carried conveniently and, as often as

the battalions halt, be placed at their head.

" I make it my earnest request to all the Generals, that, as fast as the army comes down the last mountain to enter upon the plain, they will each take their posts according to the directions given in this present order."

They had only a march of fifteen miles to get at the Turks who were separated from them by nothing but a chain of mountains. Across these there lay two roads, one over the highest part of the ridge; the other in a place where the hills were lower and the passage more easy. The Council of War, being assembled, was for taking the latter; but the King determined upon the former which was much shorter; nor did any of the Princes murmur, because he convinced them that the fate of Vienna depended upon a single moment, and that there are cases when expedition ought to be preferred to caution.

On the 9th of September the whole army was in motion. The Germans, after several attempts to draw up their cannon, despaired of success and left them in the plain. The Poles were more persevering, for Konski, Palatine of Kiovia, commander of the artillery, succeeded in getting over twenty-eight pieces and none but these were used on the day of battle.

This march, which was encumbered with all sorts of difficulties, continued for three days. Two of them passed without the King's being seen by his Polish army, which began to demand where he was with the utmost anxiety. It appeared that the King had been among the troops of the Empire, endeavoring to encourage them to battle.

The army at length drew near to the last mountain, called Kalemberg. From the top of this hill, the Christians were presented, about an hour before night, with one of the finest and most dreadful prospects of the greatness of human power — an immense plain, and all the islands of the Danube, covered with pavilions whose magnificence seemed rather calculated for an encampment of pleasure than to endure hardships of war — an innumerable multitude of horses, camels, and buffaloes; two hundred thousand men, all in motion; swarms of Tartars dispersed along the foot of the mountain in their usual confusion; the fire of the besiegers incessant and terrible, and that of the besieged such as they could possibly make; in fine, a great city, distinguishable only by the tops of the steeples, and the fire and smoke that covered it.

The besieged were immediately apprised, by signals, of the approach of the army to their relief. To have an idea of the joy that the city felt, a person must have suffered all the extremities of a long siege, and be destined with his wife and children to the sword of a merciless conqueror, or to slavery in a foreign country. But this gleam of joy was soon succeeded by fear. Kara-Mustapha, with such an army, had still reasons to expect success though he did not deserve it. The King, who was examining the disposition of his forces, said to the German Generals: "This man is badly encamped; he knows nothing of war; we shall certainly beat him." It would seem that the quick, experienced eyes of Sobieski, with that wonderful intuition of a great commander, could quickly take in and notice all the faults of an antagonist. It is well known that Marshal Villars, then ingloriously employed in the Cevennes, foretold the defeat of Tallard from the bad disposition of his troops at the battle of Hochstet, and every General who cannot prophesy in the same manner ought to give up his command.

The cannon on both sides was the prelude to the important scene of the following day, which was the 12th of September, a day that was to decide whether Vienna under Mohammed IV should have the fate of Constantinople under Mohammed II, and whether the Empire of the West should be reunited to the Empire of the East; perhaps also whether Europe should continue a Christian continent.

CHAPTER XV

A FEW hours before the break of day the King, the Duke of Lorraine and several of the Generals joined in an act of religion which was very much practiced in those days, not so much in ours. They asked the protection of the Son of God, while the Turks were invoking the one God of Abraham by repeated cries of Allah! Allah!

This cry redoubled about sunrising, when the Christian army descended from the mountain with a slow and even pace, keeping its ranks together, preceded by its cannon, and halting every few steps, to fire and load again. The front grew wider and deeper in proportion as the space enlarged. The plain was a vast amphitheater where the Turks, in the utmost agitation, beheld the motions of their enemies. It was at this time that the Cham of the Tartars bade the Vizier observe the lances adorned with streamers belonging to the Polish horse guards and said to him, " The King is at their head," words which filled him with dismay. However superior his own army was in point of numbers, he now knew that he must meet and must combat a leader who had never failed of victory.

146

The Vizier ordered the Tartars to put all their prisoners, to the number of thirty thousand, to death. These prisoners had been gathered together, in the march to Vienna, from towns and villages enroute. They were composed of all classes, rich and poor, bond and free, male and female, and of all ages. Instantly he then ordered his troops to march towards the mountain, and at the same time ordered a general assault to be made upon the place. This last order should have been given sooner, for the Christians had now recovered courage, while the Janizaries, provoked at their General, had lost it.

In the meantime the Christians were coming down and the Turks ascended to meet them, so that the action was soon begun. The first line of the Christian army, consisting wholly of foot, charged with such impetuosity that it made room for the line of cavalry which took post in the interval between the battalions. The King, the Princes and the Generals advancing to the front, fought sometimes with the horse and sometimes with the foot. The two other lines followed close upon the foremost. Konski, whose skill in military art was equal to his intrepidity in action, had the care of the artillery which was loaded with cartridge-shot, and fired at a very small distance.

The scene of this first engagement, in the ground between the plain and the mountain, was broken by vineyards, rising grounds, and little valleys. The

enemy, having left their cannon at the entrance of
the vineyards, suffered much from those of the Christians.   The combatants, being dispersed about on the
unequal ground, disputed it with great fury till towards noon when the Count de Maligni, brother to
the Queen of Poland, got possession of a rising
ground which took the Turks in flank, who, being
driven from hill to hill, retired towards the plain
and drew up along the border of their camp.

The Christian army, the left wing in particular,
transported at this success and crying out victory,
must needs push their advantages without intermis-
sion.   Their ardor was unquestionably noble but
the King thought it dangerous.   The German cavalry, being heavily mounted, would soon have been
out of wind in the distance between them and the
enemy.   A still stronger reason was that all the different bodies having been engaged, sometimes upon
rising grounds and sometimes in valleys, had inevitably fallen into some confusion and disturbed
the order of battle.

Some time therefore was taken to repair the disorder, and the plain became the scene of a triumph
which posterity will always have a difficulty to believe.   Seventy thousand men marched to attack two
hundred thousand, and the reader must keep in mind
that the Turks and Tartars were well instructed and
drilled in the art of war, and in accouterments and

in all preparations of a soldier they could not be excelled, and that they possessed qualities that made them regarded as being the best soldiers of the world. This will give the reader some sort of a conception of the daring of seventy thousand men in attacking this mighty host. In the Turkish army, the Bashaw of Diarbekir commanded the right wing, the Bashaw of Buda the left, and the Vizier was in the center, having with him the Aga of the Janizaries and the General of the Spahis.

The two armies continued motionless for some time, apparently like gladiators in the arena, each one waiting for the other to strike the first blow; the Christians in silence; the Turks and Tartars with their deafening cries accompanied by the sound of clarions. In this awful moment a red pavilion was erected in the midst of the Infidels and close to it the great standard of Mohammed, a sacred object to the professors of the Mussulman faith, like the Labarum of the Roman Emperors, or the Oriflamme of the ancient Kings of France. But this imposture, which sometimes inspires them with as much courage as Truth can give the Christians, did not do its office on this great occasion, for the Vizier had deprived it of all its virtue.

As soon as the King had given orders for the charge, the Polish cavalry, saber in hand, pushed vigorously on to the Vizier, whose post was made manifest by the standard. The first ranks were instantly forced and the Poles penetrated even to the numerous squadrons that surrounded the Vizier. The Spahis disputed the victory, but all the rest, Walachians, Moldavians, Transylvanians, Tartars and even Janizaries themselves, showed no alacrity, a fatal effect of an army's hating and despising its General. It is doubtful whether in all the world's history we have a single instance where an army that has not the most complete and thorough confidence in its General has ever been victorious, and never where they distrusted or despised their leader. The Vizier attempted to recover their good opinion by showing courage and good behavior, but he had lost his opportunity. He addressed himself next to the Bashaw of Buda and the other generals, who answered him only with a silence of despair: " And thou," said he to the Tartar Prince, " dost thou too refuse to help me? " The Cham saw no safety but in flight. The Spahis were now reduced to their last efforts. The Polish horse had broken and scattered them, and the great green standard of the Ottoman Empire disappeared, the Vizier turned his back, and his flight made the consternation universal. It was soon communicated from the center to the wings, which were hard pressed by all the divisions of the Christian army at the same time; the left by Jablonowski, the right by the Electors, while the Duke of Lorraine fell upon the center and the King animated the whole by his actions and his orders. That immense multitude which, under an able leader, ought to have surrounded and overwhelmed its enemies in so extensive a plain, was deprived by terror of all strength and presence of mind. Had night been farther off it would have been a total defeat; as things were it was only a precipitate retreat.

The King advanced next towards the Janizaries, who were left to continue the siege, but they had all disappeared and Vienna was completely delivered. The victorious troops would fain have entered the enemy's camp, allured by the immense riches that the Turks had left, but the temptation was a dangerous one at this juncture. The enemy, favored by the darkness of the night, might return and cut in pieces an army which would be too much employed in pillage to make any defense. An order was therefore issued to continue all night under arms upon pain of death.

CHAPTER XVI

ABOUT six in the morning the enemy's camp was opened to the soldiers, whose desire for plunder was at first paralyzed, as it were, by a most shocking spectacle. In several parts of the camp mothers were butchered, some of whom had their children still hanging at their breasts. These women were of good repute, not like a certain class that sometimes follows the army and are always a pest to the army and the morals of the soldiers. They were virtuous wives whom their husbands chose rather to kill than to dispose to the lusts of the Christians. The children escaped this slaughter, and five or six hundred of them were preserved, whom the Bishop of Newstadt took care of and educated in the religion of the conquerors. It seems to have been a practice for the Mohammedans to take their families with them upon these campaigns. It seems so strange as we view it from our standpoint, that they should have in this way exposed their loved ones to all the horrors and the vicissitudes of war.

Never did an army get possession of more abundant spoil; for the Turks, who are economists in time of peace, display great magnificence in the field.

The hero of the day had his share upon the present occasion. He wrote to the Queen that the Grand Vizier had made him his heir, and that he had found in his tent the value of several millions of ducats. " You will have no room," added he, " to say of me what the women of Tartary say, when their husbands return empty-handed: ' You are no men because you come back without plunder.' "

Among the many things which fell into the hands of the soldiers there were two which attracted the notice of all but excited the covetousness of none. One was a large standard which, in the hurry of joy, was taken for that of Mohammed. But this was certainly a mistake, for the singular precautions that the Turks used had always prevented this calamity. The standard is enclosed in an ark of gold with the Alcoran and the robe of the Prophet. This ark is carried by a camel which goes before the Sultan or Vizier; and, when the standard is displayed in battle, an officer of the race of Mohammed, called the Naikbul-Eschret, was appointed to watch the event of the combat; and, when the victory inclines ever so little to the side of the enemy, the guard at once disappears with all haste from the field of battle with the sacred deposirum. The Vizier, upon the present occasion, accompanied this Officer in his flight. But the Christians, who were fond of being mistaken in this fact, have persisted in declaring that they pos-

sess the famous standard; and the historians, one
after another, not excepting the celebrated author of
the Annals of the Empire, have adopted their mistake.   The other sacred implement that made part
of the booty was a picture of the Virgin found in the
Vizier's tent, with this inscription in Latin:

Per hanc imaginem victor eris, Johannes.
Per hanc imaginem victor ero Johannes.

The first line, " John, by this image thou shalt
conquer," comes from the Virgin; to which John
answers, " By this image, I, John, will conquer."
It was evidently an imitation of the sign which Constantine claims to have seen in the air when he was
marching to give battle to Maxentius.

The image gave occasion for much speculation.
Some thought it very remarkable that the Vizier
should have in his tent a presage of his approaching
ruin which ought rather to have been in King John's
possession.   Others insisted that no miraculous facts
should be admitted without an application of the test
of severe criticism.   The image, however, was placed
in a magnificent chapel, built by the Queen of Poland and the supposed standard of Mohammed was
sent to the Pope as an act of homage to the Lord of
Hosts.   All the cannon remained to the Emperor and
the Empire also.   The Turks lost a great many colors

and it is well known that colors are never surrendered but with great effusion of blood; and indeed, if we take only a transitory view of two armies disputing at first against each other, foot to foot, for six hours, a spot of ground full of eminences and vineyards, and afterwards coming to a general action, this will be sufficient to show that it could not be done without considerable loss; but this loss will, after all, be thought small and was so in effect for so great a victory.

The next day after the victory was a day of glory. Staremberg, the brave commander of the city, who had so resolutely and so gallantly and with so small a force of men, resisted the mighty hosts of the Turks for two whole months, had come to pay his respects to the deliverer of Vienna, for here King John thought he might show triumph without offending the Emporor, and entered the city over its ruins amidst the acclamations of the people. His horse could scarce get through the multitudes that fell prostrate before him, coming to kiss his feet and calling him their father, their savior, the noblest of all Princes. Vienna in this moment of joy forgot that it had a jealous master; and that master was their cowardly craven Emperor.

Leopold, who expected to have a triumph in his capital, though he had not been present at the battle, advanced by the Danube, scarce venturing to cast his eye upon the smoking ruins of so many hamlets, villages, gardens and country-seats. As he drew near the city he heard the firing of cannon, not intended for him. He was wounded to the very heart with this thought, and turning to the Count de Sintzendors, said to him: "The weakness of the counsels that you have had a share in occasions me this disgrace." These words, uttered with that imperious tone which always crushes a courtier, affected the Minister so much, it is said, that he died the next day. A minister who should die of grief at having advised a measure productive of misery to the people, would deserve tears.

The Emperor suspended his march, that he might not be a spectator of King John's triumph. A difficulty of ceremony contributed to stop him; the question was, whether an elective King had ever been present with an Emperor, and in what manner he had been received? The Duke of Lorraine, who listened only to the voice of gratitude, answered, "With open arms, if he has preserved the Empire." The Emperor was attentive only to his Imperial dignity, and gave King John to understand that he would not give him his hand, which was the reception the King of Poland expected of a Sovereign Prince. After much negotiation, the matter was settled by arranging to have the two sovereigns meet on horse-back upon the open plain.

When the moment of the interview arrived, the King of Poland, in a Polish bonnet and plume of feathers terminated by a large pearl hanging loose, clad in the same armor that he wore on the day of the battle, with a Roman Buckler, on which were engraved, "Not the actions of his ancestors, but his own," and mounted upon a stately horse with magnificent equippings, approached the Emperor with that heroic presence which nature had given him, and that air which his victory gave him a right to put on. The Emperor talked of nothing but the services done the Poles in all ages by the friendship and protection of the Emperors. At last, however, he let drop the word gratitude for the deliverance of Vienna. At this word the King, turning his horse, said to him: "Brother, I am glad that I have done you that small service." He was going to put an end to the discourse, which grew disagreeable, but he observed his son, Prince James, alight from his horse to pay his respects to the Emperor: "This is a Prince," said he, "whom I am educating for the service of Christendom." The Emperor, without saying a word, only nodded his head; and yet this was the young Prince whom he had promised to make his son-in-law. Such a picture can only be truly outlined before our later and broader visions, as free dwellers in the free country of our adoption and the true outlines of such a scene serve to make the Polish King, regal democrat as he was, a kingly sight indeed.

The King's dissatisfaction with the Emperor would naturally have induced him to return to his own dominions, after having saved the Empire. This was what the Republic intended, and the Queen desired; and this is what he should have done. But he flattered himself that Leopold, notwithstanding his strange behavior, would still perform his promises. The double hope of a match between an Archduchess and his son, and of the crown of Poland's being made hereditary in his family, which hope he had, no doubt, deservedly nurtured, supported him against the Imperial pride.

Kara-Mustapha, after his defeat, retired to Buda where he expected his fate. His being the son-in-law of Mohammed, was of great use to him, but the Sultana Valide of still greater. The Sultans have a particular respect for their mothers, even beyond what nature prescribes. As Mohammed was full of this filial respect for his mother, she suborned witnesses who were glad to gain preferment by compliances that are often common enough in courts. The disaster at Vienna was imputed to persons far less criminal than the Vizier. The Bashaw of Buda was strangled and lamented by the whole Ottoman Empire. It is true he had, on the present occasion, given up the Vizier to the arms of the Christians but such a defection scarce ever happens but to a despised or detested general. The fault, however, was inoxensable and he paid for it with his head. Three other Bashaws fell with him. The Cham of the Tartars was deposed, a punishment which he could not have deserved under another Vizier.

The same courier who was charged with these cruel orders brought the real criminal distinguished marks of his continuing still in favor; but it was upon condition of his repairing this misfortune. For, vanquished as he was, he still had an army far superior to that of the conquerors; and the lists were again opened.

CHAPTER XVII

THE King of Poland began his march on the 17th of September, to complete the destruction of his enemy, for he thought that nothing was done while anything still remained to do. He was followed by the German army, but not so numerous as it was at the battle before Vienna.

A body of some six or seven thousand Turks, all cavalry, had passed the Danube at Strigonia, in order to guard the head of the bridge belonging to that town. It was commanded by a young man who was the Bashaw, named Kara-Mehemed, born for war, full of fire, ambition, and courage, and who was resolved to deserve his fortune.

The Polish troops always encamped before the rest of the army. The King flattered himself with the hopes of crushing this handful of Turks and taking the fort of Barcan at Strigonia; but, not choosing that the Germans should share in this victory, he concealed from them his march. The 7th of October was a day of blood. The Turks being covered with a rideau, the Polish vanguard did not think them so near and was attacked before it could draw up in order of battle. Disorder and confusion instantly seized the Poles; nothing was to be seen but flying parties and heads falling by the saber. This seems to be but a reaction of what has often been known in the history of warfare. The bravest troops in the world, the best handled and the best led, will sometimes, when surprised, become panic stricken and become unmanageable and flee like cravens. An instance of this, later in the world's history, was the flight of Napoleon's old guard from the field of Waterloo.

In the midst of this disorder, the King came up with the main body of horse, but his presence did not stop the panic stricken troops. The young Bashaw redoubled his activity, and the King had scarce time to form his line. He received the Turks with firmness and even charged them in turn. But the Turks opening their ranks to inclose the whole Polish line, and being stimulated with that rage which distinguished the Mohammedans under the first Cailiffs, drove back the left wing, forced the right and penetrated the center. The Towarisz were no longer that intrepid band which, about a century before, had said to their King: "What hast thou to fear with twenty thousand lances? If the sky should fall we would keep it up with their points."

In this universal disorder, when every moment added the dying to the dead and it became equally as dangerous to retreat as to resist, the Grand-General

Jablonowski besought the King to escape with his son who fought by his side, and this was effected with the greatest difficulty.

When this battle was over, the calm that succeeded presented a deplorable scene. The Polish Nobles, who had escaped the slaughter, with downcast eyes and dejected countenance, surrounded their master in mournful silence. The German Generals also had an air of sadness; but the King knew what was in their hearts. "Gentlemen," said he, with that candor which is never found but in great minds, " I confess I wanted to conquer without you, for the honor of my own nation: I have suffered severely for it, being soundly beaten, but I will take my revenge with you, and for you. To effect this must be the chief employment of our thoughts." This eloquence of the heart is perhaps superior to all the speeches in the world.

The young Bashaw, proud of the advantage he had gained over so great a king, with an inferior force, was thinking, on his side, of gathering fresh laurels. He dispatched couriers the same night to Buda, with an account of his victory. The Grand-Vizier, without losing a moment, sent a body of twenty thousand cavalry, which arrived next day by the bridge of Strigonia, the distance being no more than eighteen miles.

The King of Poland, who had recovered his

strength by a night's rest, employed the whole following day, which was the 8th, in collecting his scattered army, and counseling it for the misfortune of yestorday, in animating it to vengeance, in combining it with the Imperial troops, and in regulating the order of battle for the morrow.

The letter he wrote to the Queen, dated this day, informing her frankly of his terrible disaster, was enough to freeze her blood. He told her that he was advancing towards the enemy and that she must expect the enemy to be defeated or bid him farewell forever.

Tekeli, who was ordered by the Vizier to advance with thirty thousand men, had not arrived on the morning of the 9th when the engagement began. Any one but the young Bashaw would have avoided an action, or at least would not have fought it. It will scarce be believed that twenty-six thousand Turks, all cavalry, and without cannon, could venture a battle against fifty thousand Christians, provided with all the advantages of infantry, cavalry and artillery. The two Bashaws of Silistria and Caramania, commanded the wings. The General, elated with his late victory and promising himself another, was in the center.

The Christian army outstretched that of the Turks, by a full half of its front, and was putting itself in motion to begin the charge, when the Turks, who were quicker, fell upon them with an impetuosity, attended with howlings, which it is impossible to describe. A torrent that tumbles from the top of a mountain's brow is neither more noisy nor more rapid. The Christians received them with such firmness that not a man lost his post and with such a terrible fire that brought men and horses to the ground. The Turks wheeled round to recover a little, and instantly returned with greater fury. It was owing to the chevaux de frize, placed at the head of the battalions of the Christian army, that they were not broken. The Turks were often on the point of succeeding and as often repulsed. Never did squadrons perform their evolutions with greater dexterity and quickness nor was the excellence of the Turkish horses ever more fully displayed.

The Bashaws that commanded the wings, both covered with blood, were made prisoners, but the General still did everything that could be expected from the most determined courage. He forced his way into the center but being wounded at length in two places with a saber, and perceiving that the strength of his troops was exhausted he thought of making his retreat.

The King of Poland, who observed his first disposition towards it, did not allow him time to execute his intention but advanced at the head of his cavalry to take him in flank and cut off his retreat. The first squadrons were already seen retiring over the bridge. The Christian army now gave a great shout in its turn and, quickening its march, extended itself in the form of a crescent and came up with the enemy.

The whole was nothing now but a scene of slaughter to the Turks, whose sole object was to fly. Some got to the bridge, but the cannon swept it from end to end; and, being built of boats, it was soon overloaded and sunk under the weight. Others ran towards the fort but the fort could hold no more and drove them back. Many threw themselves into the Danube which was covered with men and horses, but the shot reached them even here, and the river swallowed them up. A body of eighteen thousand, who would not attempt this dangerous way, stayed upon the side of the river in much greater danger. The Janazaries in the fort were spectators of this slaughter and expected this to be their fate. They made all possible signals of surrender; hung out a white flag, and for fear it should not be taken notice of, tore off the sleeves of their shirts and fastened them to the ends of their weapons. But this day was not a day of mercy. Their sentence of death was written upon their palisadoes, whereupon the Polish soldiers saw the bleeding heads of their brethren. The rage that seized them at this sight cost them fresh tears which they might easily have prevented. The

Janazaries, upon the point of being forced when they offered to surrender, made a discharge which did great execution. It was an act of mere despair in the last moment they had to live. Of the twenty-six thousand Turks that were in this engagement, only two thousand escaped before the breaking down of the bridge. The young Bashaw who would have deserved a second victory, if valor was a sufficient title to it, was one of the number.

Every circumstance of this engagement, the blood-iest of that age, was astonishing. A young war-rior, who had never been in any command, ventur-ing to combat with veteran generals and defying the hero of the age; twenty-six thousand Mohammedans fighting a pitched battle against fifty thousand Chris-tians who were upon the point of being defeated; these same Mohammedans, more than men in the beginning of the action, and less than women in the end; Christians imbruing their hands after the vic-tory in the blood of eighteen thousand men who begged for mercy; a truth which I would willingly suppress if my respect for the fidelity of history would permit it. The extraordinary courage which Mohammed manifested in the beginning of this bat-tle and in the battle of the day before, all proceeded from one man; the young Bashaw of Buda who was youthful, ambitious and filled with enthusiasm; he electrified his army. This was entirely the reverse of former contests and he almost snatched victory from the jaws of defeat.   It is one of the marvels of history.

The taking of Strigonia put an end to the campaign and the armies separated.   The Poles, before they could reach their native land, had a march of hundreds of miles.   Christiana, then at Rome, wrote to the Conqueror that he had " made her feel, for the first time, the passion of envy, for she really grudged him the glorious title of deliverer of Christendom." This was the ex-Queen Christiana of Sweden, the daughter of the great Gustavus Adolphus, one of the greatest soldiers of his day and the champion of Protestant Europe; but his erratic daughter who succeeded him finally, after many misadventures, resigned her crown and entered the Catholic church and went to live and die at Rome.

The scene ended tragically on the side of the Turks.   The deposition of the Cham of Tartary, and the sacrifice of four Bashaws immediately after the affair at Vienna, was not sufficient to appease the murmurs of the Ottoman Empire.   Tekeli was sent to Constantinople, bound hand and foot.   Kara-Mustapha was strangled and his head carried to Constantinople, a fitting end to the General who had no sense of shame; a brute by nature, and possessed of very few qualities of manhood, who owed his elevation to favoritism alone.

CHAPTER XVIII

THE King passed the winter of 1684 at Cracow where he received the congratulations of Europe. But in the opinion of the Republic, he had done nothing if he did not retake Kamieniec. Having, accordingly, put himself at the head of the army, he advanced towards Jaslowiecz, a town which was the second in Podolia, before the Turks had made themselves masters of that fine province. They had set fire to the town and left nothing standing but the castle, a fortification of immense bulk, composed of eight large towers, and situated upon a rock which is made a peninsula by the River Janows. The Poles soon carried this fort which had a garrison of five hundred and thirty Janizaries and thirteen pieces of cannon. The King continued his march along the Niester, with the design of throwing a bridge over that river and entering Moldavia, in order to hinder the Turks from having any communication with Kamieniec. The whole plan was disconcerted by the great diligence of the enemy. The Poles had scarce begun work upon their bridge before twenty thousand Turks and a greater number of Tartars appeared on the other side of the river. It was not possible to throw a bridge over the river in their presence but the Tartars did not want one to get at the Poles. They surrounded the Polish army and harassed it on all sides without ever coming to action, being equally quick in running away as coming on, and always ready to repass the river if they found themselves forced to it.

In the meantime, Kamieniec, the object of this campaign, was secured from all attempts, and the Polish army suffered much in a country that was entirely deserted. To lay siege, in proper form, to a place of such strength, where there was a garrison of ten thousand men and in the presence of a superior army, was a thing impossible. The King resolved therefore, if nothing more could be done, to erect a citadel against Kamieniec, in order to pave the way for its fall at a more favorable time. He chose for this purpose, at a distance of about three miles, a rock that stood by itself upon the bank of the same river that runs by Kamieniec and not far from the Niester. The fort was completed in six weeks; a garrison was put into it and annoyed the town greatly, during the whole time that it continued in possession of the enemy; for no supplies could be received but at the hazard of a battle or struggle.

The King, not pleased with his expedition, formed a plan for letting Poland enjoy at least a taste of the sweets of peace in the midst of war, the end of

which could not be foreseen. Instead of going to enjoy the amusements of the capital he took up his
residence upon the frontiers and while he restrained
the Tartars, who are always ready for invasions, the
Nobles enjoyed their fortunes, the merchants carried on their trade, the lands were cultivated and
the peasants got bread.

At the opening of the next campaign, in 1685, the
King proposed in Council to resume the project of
the preceding year, which was to enter Moldavia,
in order to force the Hospodar to declare in favor
of Poland and make use of his assistance to take
Kamieniec. The recovery of this bulwark would
have made the nation forget all the miseries of so
long a war. The army was already assembling, but
a disorder detained the King. The Grand-General
Jabolonowski readily undertook the charge of all
that might happen.

While the army was upon its march, the King received a piece of intelligence that struck him with
amazement. The Archduchess whom Leopold had
promised to Prince James was married to the Elector of Bavaria; and the King guessed from that what
he was to expect from the other promise which re-
lated to the securing of the crown of Poland in his
family, by the intrigues, the money and the power of
the court of Vienna. Being naturally warm and
impetuous, he had great difficulty to restrain his re-

sentment till the end of the campaign and then take his measures as events would happen.

The army had already got through two-thirds of the Bucovine, a forest ninety miles long and as many broad, when the enemy appeared. The two armies drew up in order of battle with a defile between them. The march was by no means equal, for forty thousand Turks and as many Tartars were detached to seize the passes behind the Polish army and cut off their retreat. The Tartars were already seen in places that they never before approached; the inhabitants of the country took refuge in the towns and the towns expected to be forced. The alarm increased like a torrent till it reached Zolkiew, a place not far from the frontiers where the King resided for the recovery of his health. Though he was still in a weak condition, he put himself at the head of the Nobility of the neighboring provinces and some Lithuanian troops which, coming from a great distance, could not join the army in time. But the catastrophe was over before the King came. Jablonowski, after he had been fifteen days in this dismal situation, formed a plan for a retreat which seemed impracticable. Behind him there was a wood of alders which grew in a morass deep enough to swallow up men and horses. He ordered his men to take hatchets and cut down the trees close by each other, with the branches uppermost. By this means he formed two bridges wide enough for five wagons to pass in front.

The baggage began to file off, in the beginning of the night, between the eighth and ninth of October. The cavalry followed next and by break of day there remained only fifteen squadrons. The infantry and dragoons, with part of the cannon, came in the rear, and were commanded by Konski, General of the artillery, a man whom it was impossible to surprise and who had distinguished himself in an illustrious manner at the battle of Vienna.

The Turks at length poured out of the great wood that was in front of the Polish army. The cavalry began the attack and charged with its usual impetuosity, but was so roughly handled that it retired into the wood again to make room for fresh squadrons. The charge was repeated in this manner ten or twelve times, and the different bodies succeeded each other so fast that the Poles had scarce time to load again. The fire-arms on both sides were no longer depended upon; the Turkish saber and the Polish battle-ax were to decide the point. On both sides there was an equal degree of fury and true courage, but the Poles fought with better conduct. A body of between eleven and twelve thousand men had been engaged for ten hours against forty thousand. All the different bodies supported each other like the bastions of a movable fortress. Never was any man possessed of cooler valor than Konski. The officers and soldiers cried out to him to take care of himself for the common good: " I have not yet received a wound," he answered, " and I see some of you fighting with several." His behavior in this action gave the nation so high an opinion of him that, at the death of the King, later on, he was named among the candidates for the throne and would have been elected had it not been for the fatal mistake of permitting foreign Princes to be named for the Polish throne, to which his virtues gave him a fair claim. He was, however, contented with living and dying first Senator and the laurels which he acquired, on this occasion will continue fresh to the end of time. As the night drew on, the retreat was completed, the enemy appearing no more. The rear joined the cavalry which, during the whole action, was drawn up in battle in a little plain beyond the wood of alders, expecting all the while to be attacked by the Tartars who were within view. After all, if Konski had the honor of executing this celebrated retreat, Jablonowski had the glory of having planned it when it seemed impracticable.

Jablonowski kept the field for three weeks longer at the head of the invasion of the Tartars. The Polish arms acquired great glory but no real advantage in this campaign. The Moldavians were not subdued; Kamieniec continued in the hands of the

Turks, and the whole design of the armament miscarried.

The King returned to Zolkiew, where he endeavored to regain his health, not by that delicate and cautious way of living which serves only to prolong a state of weakness, but by following the diversion of the chase. It has always been said that hunting is the image of war. In most parts of Europe this image represents its object of a very small size; but Poland increases its magnitude in imitation of the Asiatic sovereigns who hunt with a complete army. The King kept in pay five hundred Janizaries, all real Turks, taken in battle, armed and dressed in their former manner. A circular space was marked out for them in a forest, which they encompassed with nets, leaving an opening that answered to the plain. At a considerable distance, a line of dogs held in leashes formed a crescent; behind which the King, huntsmen and the spectators were drawn up in another line. The signal being given, other dogs were let loose into the forest and drove before them whatever they found. In a short time there came out stags, elks, auroxes (a sort of wild bull of singular beauty, strength, and fierceness), lynxes, boars and bears, and every species of dogs attacked the beast that was its proper prey. The beasts could neither get back to the forest nor stay by the nets, because the Janizaries were posted there to prevent it. The huntsmen did not engage in the combat, but when the dogs were likely to be overpowered. This mixed multitude of men, horses, and wild beasts, the noise of horns, the variety of combats, and all this apparatus of war, set out with proper magnificence, struck the natives of the south, who were present at it, with surprise; nor did the Republic murmur at the expense, because it was not defrayed out of the public coffers.

Hunting, however, was not the King's sole amusement. As the Diet was not to be assembled this year (1686), and it was uncertain whether the war would be renewed or not, he had much leisure upon his hands. The very recreations of a laborious king are a public benefit. The pleasure of building happening to strike his fancy he pitched upon a delightful situation on the banks of the Vistula, about six miles from Warsaw. A Villa now rose out of the ground and the north was ornamented with the architecture of Italy. But the satisfaction the King enjoyed in raising this edifice did not make him forget his resentment against Leopold, and he showed it by declaring a resolution to quit the league. Leopold saw that it was necessary to present him with some other promise to keep him steady, and proposed to him the conquest of Moldavia and Walachia to be possessed as a sovereignty by his family, promising him a body of German troops which should advance from the banks of the Danube to assist him in the reduction of those provinces.

This double crown was a strong temptation to the King. On the other side, Mohammed, who daily sustained fresh losses, made him an offer, if he would quit the league, to restore Kamieniec with a considerable sum of money, to indemnify Poland for the expenses of so long a war.

CHAPTER XIX

IN this competition between the Republic and his own family the King was not able to decide or did not make the proper choice. He was prevailed upon by the Jesuits, who controlled the Queen, and the voice of paternal affection, to decide in favor of his family and leave to fortune the interests of Poland. However, he disguised his real design in this expedition under the specious pretense of conquering only for the Republic, and of recovering Kamieniec in a more glorious manner by cutting off all its succors, since it received none from any other quarter but Moldavia.

It was a long time since Poland had seen so fine and so numerous an army. It amounted to nearly forty thousand fighting men. When it crossed the Bucovine, a place where it was on the point of perishing in the preceding campaign, they threw bridges over all the passes which could either retard their march or hinder their return. The reigning Prince of Moldavia was Constantine Cantemir. He did not stay to surrender, till the army was at the gates of his capital, it was scarce got out of the Bucovine when a nobleman arrived from his court who told the King that his master thought himself happy in

the prospect of being soon delivered from the Ottoman yoke, to enter into the obedience of Poland; that
he regretted his not being able to come in person to
wait upon so great a king; and that his view in stay-
ing for him in his capital was to hinder the people
from leaving it.

The King, charmed with a conquest which would
occasion the shedding of no tears, hastened his march
to the plain of Cetzora, where the army halted.
This plain recalled to his mind the slaughter and the
glory of his grandfather, by presenting him with a
view of the intrenchments where the famous Zolkiewski, with thirty thousand Poles, repulsed an
army of a hundred thousand Turks and Tartars, and
of the pyramid, which was still standing, where the
names of that hero addressed the passenger in these
animating words: " Learn of me, how sweet and
how honorable it is to die for one's country," a
maxim that was engraved upon the King's heart
from his earliest youth.

When the King approached the town, he was met
by the principal inhabitants, but was surprised at not
seeing the Hospodar.   Cantemir's situation was extremely critical.   One of his sons was an hostage at
Constantinople, with four nobles of the country as
pledges for his fidelity; and on the other hand, a
Christian army was ready to fall upon him without
his having any hope from the Turkish forces which

were, at this juncture, at too great a distance to defend him. He had recourse, therefore, to a pretended submission, in order to engage the conqueror to spare his dominions, and, to exculpate himself with the Porte, he took refuge with his family and treasures in the Turkish army which was encamped near the mouth of the Danube. His flight was not disagreeable to the King who, as he resolved to keep his conquests, would have been puzzled how to dispose of the Hospodar; but he was displeased at his having carried over his troops to the enemy. He learned, from the Moldavians themselves, that he was the worst prince that had for a long time governed that country; that having bought his crown at a very dear rate, he was a professed usurer, and behaved in the most oppressive manner and that the very moment of his flight had been distinguished by acts of extortion which exceeded the ordinary measure of his rapaciousness.

While these things were in this situation in Moldavia, the Walachians were far from being in a state of tranquillity. Fear, and still more, the humanity of the victor, which was loudly celebrated by fame, induced them to submit and they obliged their Hospodar to send him a deputation, declaring that their gates were open.

The King, being now master of Moldavia and Walachia, extended his views still farther. Before him lay the ancient Bessarabia, now called Budziac, and all that vast country which lies between the Danube and the Niester, up to the coast of the Black Sea. The Crimea itself tempted his ambition; he was pleased with the idea of chastising the Tartars upon their own ground and seemed to intend opening himself a passage even to Constantinople by ways which were deemed impracticable. He therefore resumed his march without quitting the Pruth, the water of which was necessary for the subsistence of the army in so dry a season; and, besides this, was very wholesome and mitigated a dysentery that raged among the troops.

When the Poles came to Gallacz, a town not far from the place where the Pruth falls into the Danube, the plain was covered with a confused multitude of Tartars, and, soon after, the Turks made their appearance in good order. The King looked towards the Danube, whence he expected the succor which the Emperor had promised him, but Leopold, attentive only to his own interests, was pushing his successes in Hungary. The King, finding himself deceived, felt all the danger to which he had exposed himself. He had been upon the march full three months and must now force his way through fresh troops, superior to his own by more than half their number. The only resource left him was to retreat and this could be done only by weathering a storm for two months together before he reached the port; and, if he did not gain any great advantage over his enemies in this campaign, he at least kept them at bay with inferior forces.

A diet was to be assembled in 1687, but the Senate put it off to save expenses at a time when the continuation of the war was so heavy a burden. The nation, however, though not assembled in form, murmured greatly at the projects of its chief. His plan for the ensuing campaign was to secure his conquest of Moldavia by carrying his victorious arms quite to the Black Sea. To execute this design, it was necessary that he should continue steadfast in the league, notwithstanding his dissatisfaction with the Emperor, to the end that the Turks, being attacked on all quarters, might be more easily dispossessed of their territories on the side of Poland. But Poland began to suspect that these great projects were calculated for the benefit of his own family more than for that of the nation, and those who had no doubt that this was his intention observed in an angry strain that it was maintaining a war of which there would be no end; and aiming at distant objects while the enemy was suffered to continue undisturbed at the gates of the Kingdom in a fortress which it was a disgrace not to retake. The King could not help feeling that the complaints were just; and the bombardment of Kamieniec was resolved on.

The army began its march about the end of June. The King attended the expedition in a languid and exhausted state. It had now been more than thirty years since he went upon the field, and those years had been spent almost continuously in the hardships and exposures and tumults of war, in which he had been the principal and responsible actor, and his magnificent frame and splendid constitution, which had been supplemented by a temperate and well regulated life, had begun to give way before the demands that had been made upon him. His mind had lost nothing of its former vigor; it was his body that was losing its strength and he collapsed entirely at Jaslowiecz where he was obliged to give up the command and Prince James took possession of it with all the ensigns of power. The Prince, therefore, taking the thunderbolt out of his father's hands, advanced towards Kamieniec, where he arrived on the 10th of July. The bombardment lasted six days, with a most terrifying noise. The besiegers played upon the town with fifty pieces of cannon and sixteen mortars and the besieged returned their fire from three hundred. The Poles soon discovered that their powder was being consumed to little purpose, and therefore slackened their fire when they saw the Tartars pass the Niester and advance towards them. However, nothing decisive happened between the two armies, which only cannonaded each other across the river with little loss. The campaign ended with no other exploit than the ruin of a few houses in Kamieniec and the death of three or four hundred Tartars who fell into an ambuscade; inconsiderable effects to be produced by so great a cause.

CHAPTER XX

THE efforts of the league were attended with success in other places; but the King, when he was informed of the horrid tragedy that the Austrians had enacted in Hungary, repented that he had not set that crown upon the head of his son, when the Hungarians, won by his virtues, solicited him to do it after the battle of Vienna. He observed too that his health was decaying and hoped at least to transmit to him that which he wore himself and resolved to take advantage of the approaching Diet to make the Poles concur in his design, but this Diet afforded only a scene of distraction.

At the same time, however (1688), a scene of more joyful sort was preparing for the King at Wilna, the capital of Lithuania, a city which, having never seen its sovereign, was impatient to pay him its homage. The people took no part in quarrels of state; they were attentive only to the glory and the benevolent disposition of their sovereign and left it to the Grandees to criticise his faults. He was received upon the road, and in that great city with those acclamations and signs of joy which are never extorted from a free people against their will.

From Wilna he repaired to Warsaw, where the Queen was impatient to see him, as much for the pleasure of sharing with him in the government, as for the love she bore him. She prevailed upon him to submit to a course of medicine before he took up arms and to concert measures for marrying Prince James to a widow whose immense possessions were covered all over Europe. This widow was the heiress of the house of Radziwil, the same Prince James would have married once before in the year 1680, and which he lost by means of the Elector of Brandenburg, who procured her for his son, Prince Louis. The young husband did not long enjoy his acquisition, and the Court of Poland negotiated at Berlin to get possession of the widow, with greater hopes of success than ever. The treaty was already far advanced and the Polish envoy sent word that Prince James' presence was necessary to insure success. The Prince flew to Berlin, entered the town incognito, and had a conference with the French minister, who was ordered by his master to promote the match with a view to taking off King John from the interests of the House of Austria. He had a private interview with the young widow and got from her a formal promise to marry him in eight months (by which time the conventional period of mourning would be out), upon pain of forfeiting her entire fortune. The marriage-presents were given and received on each side and the Prince set out for Warsaw, perfectly satisfied with his success. In consequence of this match he would be in possession of four duchies in the heart of Poland, acquire great personal weight and be a considerable step nearer to the throne.

The news of the Prince's success was received with great joy by the Court of Warsaw, and particularly by the King, who loved his son tenderly and stood in great need of laying his heart open to the impressions of joy. But it was only a transitory gleam, which was soon to be followed by grief. While Prince James was returning home with his promise, a more fortunate rival actually married the lady at Berlin. The husband was Prince Charles of Newburg, third son to the Elector Palatine, and brother to the Empress. The Elector of Brandenburg, to whom Leopold held out the alluring object of a regal crown, favored this act of treachery, if the ill offices, which the maxims of politics have sanctified, if the morality of sovereigns can be called by that name. It was still the Emperor Leopold who thwarted all the views of his ally, the King of Poland, who had saved him from destruction.

This mortifying blow was received by the Court of Poland with all the transports of grief and revenge. If John had been master of a force equal to that of Leopold or Louis XIV, he would not have been affronted with impunity in the person of his son. As things were, he submitted to the only expedient he had left, and acted as his weakness, and indeed wisdom itself, required. He consulted the Polish lawyers concerning the promise given by the faithless princess, and the penalty to which she had subjected herself. They were of the opinion that the King had a right to confiscate all her estates, but such a sentence could be pronounced only by the tribunal of the nation assembled in a general diet, and the nation was, at this juncture, wholly intent upon war. The negotiation of Berlin, and the weak state of the King's health, put off, till the month of August, the opening of the campaign, which was attended with no success.

The King could not quit his designs upon the two crowns of Moldavia and Walachia, which he hoped to leave to his family, if that of Poland should pass into other hands. The report that he was so much taken up with this great object as to forget Kamieniec gained credence, and therefore he gave affront to the whole nation, and helped create dissatisfaction with his administration.

The year 1687 began and ended in sorrow, but the King had a larger share of it than his subjects. A Diet in which all his views proved abortive; the miscarriage of his attempts upon Kamieniec; a drouth that desolated the kingdom; the jealousies of oppo-

site factions; the dissensions that reigned among all
the orders of the state; all these circumstances filled
his mind with melancholy.

He was also accused of aiming at absolute power.
There was not much to sustain such a suspicion,
though doubtless there were great temptations to do
so. The great king had come to realize the utter
hopelessness of maintaining the power of Poland and
continuing her a great power, with her absurd constitution. There are only two forms of government
that have any right to exist, and one is an absolute
monarchy, where all is invested in the hands of a
sovereign, and the other is a pure democracy. The
latter is always preferable, but such form of government as Poland possessed was the most unfortunate
of all: A republic where the great mass of the people had no voice; where the governor was in power
with the nobility; with the ambitions and the intrigues of the nobility, there was nothing in it but
weakness. The King, no doubt, saw this and I believe had tried to remedy this evil rather than to
obtain a permanent crown for his family. Some
indications of a desire for absolute power undoubtedly manifested themselves to the over-suspicious;
but, if he was seriously bent upon it, is it credible
that he would have called together the Diet so often?
He could not be ignorant that when a nation is assembled it is always superior to its chief, but he pre-

ferred the interests of the Republic much more than his own authority and this was manifest from the fact that no other sovereign consulted the nation so often by calling together its Diet as he did.

CHAPTER XXI

THE approach of the winter of 1691 gave time to the princes of the Christian league to form new plans and recover their strength. The King of Poland was still hesitating between Leopold and Louis XIV. His reputation in Europe was the greatest of all the European sovereigns, but his power was much less and, therefore, he endeavored to keep terms with them both. His inclinations were for France, but his interest again determined him to side with the House of Austria. France indeed did not fail to make him tempting offers, but the House of Austria, by being so near his dominions, was in a condition to fulfill the promises it gave whenever it was disposed to keep its word, but there remained the annoying fact that it never kept its word with the King, and yet, in spite of all this, by some fatality which is not understood, the King of Poland was still disposed toward Leopold. The King, at this very juncture, had a family concern to settle with that court. He wanted to marry his son, Prince James; and there was no fit match for him in Poland, since that kingdom had lost its richest heiress. France, indeed, might have offered a princess of the blood, but it was resolved to have the daughter of a sovereign; and Leopold proposed a daughter of the Elector of Palatine. She was sister to that very Charles of Newburg, of whom Prince James had so much cause to complain. By this marriage the house of Sobieski became allied to all the crowns of Europe, and Prince James was brother-in-law to the Emperor. This was the first instance of the Emperor's having dealt sincerely with the King of Poland, and even in this he consulted rather his own ends than those of his ally whom he fixed more firmly than ever in his interest by this new connection.

The Emperor being thus appeased and the French faction humbled, the marriage rejoicings were resumed with great splendor, when all was again disturbed by the disagreement that rose in the royal family. The Queen of Poland, who still ruled in her husband's heart, had a mind to make the Princess of Poland sensible of her power; the latter was not so tractable as the former expected; Prince James, let it be said to his credit and honor, in this unfortunate family dissension in the most chivalrous manner took sides with his young wife.

His brother, Prince Alexander, was now no longer a child, and began to fix his eyes upon the splendors of the throne. The charms that accompany the first bloom of youth, an open countenance, an agreeable figure, a graceful air, and gentle manners, had gained

for him the heart of his mother; and his obedience
to her, in all of her whims and desires, probably had
more to do with this than anything else. Even the
nation was already prepossessed in his favor; and it
is the nation that makes the king. It was a saying
current in the kingdom, that the youngest was the
son of the King, and the eldest the son of the Grand-
Marshal. Besides, as the letter "J" had been
found in the collection of the Polish prophecies to
point out King John: the letter "A" was now discovered to begin the name of his successor.

Prince Alexander was, therefore, considered as a
rival by Prince James, whose jealousy rose to a
higher pitch than ever when the King left Warsaw
on the 13th of June, 1691, and took with him this
favorite son to present him to the army and form him
for military glory, and yet the elder son could not
complain of being slighted by his august father.
The King had invited him to accompany him with
the Princess of Poland, till the expedition was ended.
But Prince James, who was dissatisfied with everything in his present fit of ill humor, answered that
he would not expose his wife to the harsh treatment
of the Queen and that as to himself, having no settled revenue, he could not bear the expense of the
campaign. He thought proper to conceal the true
reason and the King, who might have laid his commands upon him, left him to his own inclinations

and departed without him.

The next day the Prince was still more uneasy, and, having advised the Austrian ambassador, gave notice to the Grand-Chancellor that he would leave the kingdom if Prince Alexander continued his journey; nor will Poland, added he, disapprove of my retiring when I shall inform the public, in a manifesto, that the King intends the throne for the younger son, in prejudice of his elder. It is possible that the Queen had formed this project at this time. The whole life of the Queen, since she became the wife of the King, had been one of constant intrigue, supplemented always by the Jesuit priest who was constantly in court to do her bidding. But the King certainly never thought of it, and had he been at all prejudiced in favor of his younger sons at an age when the dispositions of the mind do not yet unfold themselves, it is probable he would have leaned toward Prince Constantine, the youngest, who was his very picture. But Prince James' passion would suffer him to attend to nothing.

The King ordered him to be told that he might set out with a father's curse attending him whenever he pleased; but that he must never expect to see his sovereign and his father. This menace had no effect upon the Prince, who answered that he was going to retire to the Netherlands, of which Spain had offered him the government. The King was highly exasperated and had thoughts of punishing him; his punishment had already begun, for the couriers dared not visit him and even his friends forsook him. The Jesuit Vota and the Venetian Resident, both of them eloquent and insinuating, endeavored in a private conference to convince him of the weakness of his jealousy against his brother whose tender age entitled him to a few empty caresses; of the injustice of his suspicions with regard to the succession to the crown; and of the enormity and the danger of rebelling against his father and King. They prevailed upon him to ask pardon and told him that he would be very happy if he could obtain it. The Prince, therefore, went to the army to throw himself at the King's feet. The father soon forgave him and permitted him to share the laurels which he expected to gather at this campaign. It was an affecting sight to see the hero between his two sons, one restored to favor and already inured to arms; the other already beloved and going to learn the way to conquest and all three marching against the enemies of their country. The Queen and the Princess of Poland stayed behind upon the frontier and, womanlike, concealed their mutual aversion.

It was resolved in the council of war held by the Poles to enter Walachia, as the siege of Kamieniec still appeared impracticable with their present forces, to make themselves masters by the way of Soroc, a

Turkish fortress upon the Niester. In effect, Soroc and Nerzecum were all the fruit of the campaign. The vast quantity of snow which fell uncommonly early, froze the soldiers, broke up the roads, embarrassed the artillery and the wagons, and fatigued both men and horses. When the Polish army arrived upon the frontiers of the kingdom they looked as if they had come from a defeat. This was the fourth time that the King failed in his attempts upon Moldavia and Walachia, and the Emperor Leopold wanted but little of being equally or more unfortunate in Hungary.

This campaign was the last that the King of Poland ever made. It was not his advanced age that made it necessary for him to retire (for he was only sixty-one), but forty years spent in war, during which he never spared his own person; ten in the great offices of the Republic; eighteen upon a throne which required constant action; all these labors had worn out his body and his mind felt the effects of it. He resigned the command of the army to the Grand-General Jablonowski, in order to apply himself wholly to the internal administration of the kingdom, and even this was above his strength. He was in the ambiguous situation of being too far gone to govern himself and not far enough to be wholly governed by others.

CHAPTER XXII

THE time drew near when the King of Poland was to end his reign, his life, and his sufferings. It was now four years since he had given up the command of the army; he had lately quitted the frontier, where his presence kept the enemy in awe, and fixed his residence at Warsaw on account of his health. He labored at the same time under the effects of his old wounds, the gout, the gravel, many symptoms of the dropsy, and a great difficulty of breathing; and it was uncertain by which he would fall. He daily lost some portion of that ethereal fire which animates the human frame; nor could the furs in which he lay wrapped upon the couch restore him either motion or spirits.

The Turks and Tartars had some knowledge of his condition, but they considered him as a lion, to whom the other animals showed respect, even when he is asleep. They attempted nothing of importance, at a time when they might have done what they pleased; only a few Tartars made their incursions which were restrained by the Grand-General Jablonowski.

A circumstance still more extraordinary is that the King's illness contributed also to save the nation from its own madness. Being just upon the point of losing him, its attention was more taken up with the thoughts of a future leader than with the divisions that had disturbed its peace for the three last years. They who carried their views beyond their own country were divided between the Electors of Bavaria and Saxony and the Prince of Conti. They who were for choosing at home, mentioned Joblonowski or Konski; the partisans of the present royal family talked of Prince James or Prince Alexander. The King, in the few easy moments that his disease left him, had a prospect of nothing but misfortunes; his kingdom disturbed by factions within, and attacked by enemies without; the crown, which he had gained by merit and worn with glory, just going to become a prey to factions; uncertain whether it would continue in his family, and that family, by separating into different interests, completing the anxieties of his mind. In this situation he gave up everything to fortune, and, next to the consolations of religion, had recourse to letters and philosophy for mitigating the evils he felt.

During the whole winter of 1696 weekly reports of his death were spread over Europe and Asia. At the approach of spring the increasing warmth of the sun seemed to revive in him a few sparks of life, and he went to his fine gardens at Villanow to breathe a purer air, but, alas! he was too far gone to enjoy it.

On the 17th day of June, being Sunday, the King took a walk in his garden at Villanow. He even dined with some appetite, and showed other symptoms of being better; but death was busy within him all the while. A few hours after he was seized with a fit of apoplexy, in the midst of the royal family, and fell motionless upon the floor. In about an hour he recovered his senses, and, regretting as it were, being waked out of this sleep of death, in which he was insensible of the miseries of life, he said in a language that was familiar to him, " Stave bena "— I was well. Every face but his own was frozen with terror. He bore his sufferings with the firmness of a soldier, a philosopher and a Christian; and employed his last moments in endeavoring to convince his children of the necessity of their living in the closest union. He conjured the Queen to have no other interest in view but theirs, if she desired to preserve the crown in her family, recommending them all to follow the advice of Polignac who had merited, he said, their confidence and his. He exhorted also the Senators who were present to preserve mutual concord for the good of the Republic, whose welfare would be an object of his wishes, even in the presence of the great source of all power, before whom he should so soon appear; and he died, like Augustus, on the same day of the year that he was raised to the throne, in the sixty-sixth year of his age, and the twenty-third of his reign.

Those who hated and those who envied the King of Poland gave him, even before his death, the name of Vespasian. If he had one of the Emperor's faults, the love of money, he was also possessed of his virtues. Like him, he was raised to the throne by his military services. The charms of his wit, the readiness with which he spoke several languages, his acquaintance with polite literature, the agreeableness of his conversation, the gentleness of his manners, his sincerity in friendship, his conjugal tenderness and paternal affection — all these qualities, which would have made him an amiable man in private life, would have been sufficient for his exalted station. Endued with great strength of body and activity of mind, deeply read in the laws of his country, acquainted with the interest of foreign nations, and versed in the theory of war, equally eloquent in the Diet and enterprising in the field, he convinced his countrymen, before he was raised to the throne, of his capacity to govern and defend them. He possessed, in an eminent degree, most of the virtues that become a royal station. He did justice to his enemies, as well as to his friends; and always behaved to the latter in the same manner as when he wanted their assistance to gain the crown. The warmth of his temper made him soon take fire; but his heart was void of malice. His cruelty to the Turks, after a victory, must be attributed to a remnant of the crusading spirit, which, upon these occasions, and these only, soured the natural humanity of his temper, which was not sufficiently matured by philosophy. He was often affronted in such a state as Poland, where liberty is always upon the watch against the hand that governs; and yet he never lifted up that hand but against those who offended their country. His zeal for religion was free from the acrimony of an intolerating spirit; Greeks, Protestants, Jews, and some remains of the Socinians, lived in peace under his government; and this was no small matter, at a time when other Catholic powers were banishing or massacring their subjects in order to convert them. The dignity of a king did not obliterate from his mind the principles of a citizen, and he assembled the nation much oftener than any of his predecessors. He spent his reign in the Senate, in the midst of Diets, and in the fatigues of war; he never thought that the palace of a king should be appropriated to magnificence and luxury; but made himself thoroughly acquainted with men and things. In concerting the plan of his campaigns, he listened to every one, but was determined by himself alone, and, knowing how necessary the presence of a king is, for the purpose of discipline, celerity and even victory, he always headed his troops in person till the ill condition of his health prevented him. His country always admired, and would perhaps have loved him, if a free people were not always jealous of their liberty; perhaps, too, if he had been less fond of the Queen. He had the singular glory of humbling the Ottoman power, which for a long time had humbled the Princes of Christendom. All Europe sought his alliance, and Poland acquired an importance under his government that it never possessed afterwards. Charles XII, the Alexander of the North, lamented his death in these emphatic terms: "So great a king ought never to have died."

This book is DUE on the last date stamped below

Form L-9-35m-8,'28

Made in the USA
Thornton, CO
07/30/23 23:42:44

75c8f045-de20-4d86-a2c3-e4aed97e5bfbR01